The
Joseph D. and Mary E. Jose

Collection of Biography and History

**PURCHASED FROM FUNDS
GIVEN IN GRATEFUL MEMORY BY
THEIR CHILDREN TO**

The Library of Mount Union College

Immortal Village

DONALD CULROSS PEATTIE

Immortal Village

WOODBLOCK ILLUSTRATIONS BY PAUL LANDACRE

UNIVERSITY OF CHICAGO PRESS · CHICAGO

UNIVERSITY OF CHICAGO PRESS · CHICAGO 37

Agent: CAMBRIDGE UNIVERSITY PRESS · LONDON

COPYRIGHT 1945 BY THE UNIVERSITY OF CHICAGO. ALL RIGHTS RESERVED
PUBLISHED 1945. FIFTH IMPRESSION 1945. COMPOSED AND PRINTED
BY THE UNIVERSITY OF CHICAGO PRESS, CHICAGO, ILLINOIS, U.S.A.

Immortal Village grew out of a privately printed volume called
Vence, written by Donald Culross Peattie in 1926, published in
France, but not circulated other than in France. The edition of
Vence was five hundred copies. Some portions of *Vence* were
used in a book called *Happy Kingdom*, written by Donald
Culross and Louise Redfield Peattie, published by Blackie
& Son, Ltd., in Glasgow, Scotland. *Immortal Village* is a com-
pletely revised edition of *Vence*, including a new biographical
preface written by Mr. Peattie. Jacket by Paul Landacre. Cover
by Clarence Pontius from wood engraving by Paul Landacre.

Introduction

IT IS THE CUSTOM, I BELIEVE, FOR AN OLDER WRITER to introduce the work of one younger and less known. Certainly no one was ever closer to the author of this little book than I, or can better explain the circumstances under which he wrote it, since he was myself. So I take the liberty of presenting the work of a man considerably my junior who was enjoying, in a forgotten corner of Provence in 1929, all the obscurity he could use. I cannot cloak the faults of his style; indeed I am often amused by them and as editor I restrain my blue pencil with difficulty. I repress an impulse to say, "See here, young fellow, I'll show you how that passage ought to be written." But I know his answer: "You may be you—that's to be seen—but I am I. My style's my face. You may not like it, but I'll not let you add fifteen years to it."

Thus disrespectfully rebuked, I have confined most of my emendations to matters of historical fact (for I really do know a little more than he could then) and have abandoned his style to the man-eating critics whose fins I can already discern circling his frail raft.

Under the title of *Vence, the Story of a Provençal Town through Five Thousand Years*, the original edition of two hundred copies was printed at Nice, in the autumn of 1930. Until now this little book has never been sold in the United States, and the only example in public files is one in the Library of Congress, which owes its presence there, if I remember rightly, to the fact that its author sent a copy to that illimitable ossuary of authors. There has since been, I am told, a slight movement of the original edition in the rare-book trade, where the few copies adrift in this country have sold at a price that would have paid the young author's rent for a month, could he have touched the proceeds.

Pocketing them myself, I have been stopped from a smug satisfaction at the list price of bubble reputation by the reflection that the book may have been bought, rather, as a typographical curiosity. For it was set up by a French printer who knew no English. The errors on the galley proofs having been called to his attention, he removed the offending characters and inserted whatever others he had in surplus at the moment. These in turn being corrected on the page proofs, he committed to the bound copies a third crop of errors more generous than any that had preceded it. Little wonder if the venturesome small volume became an "item."

That it ever saw print is due to the kindness of Mr. William Moncreiffe, whose friendship I gained through the manuscript pages, and who offered to see them to private publication, for he too loved Vence, having a beautiful home there on the other side of the town from our countrified villa. In the pleasant philanthropy of publishing my slight history, he was joined by his friend Mr. McCoy of Grasse, and I take this occasion, when the work they godfathered appears in more dignified dress, to give thanks for their kindly offices.

But the chief purpose of these introductory pages is to explain why I draw this little work forth from the shadows of years ago and far away, in this hour of Europe's agony, while her future is still dark with doubt and threat. I do so precisely because I believe that the story of a European village, from its just conceivable Neolithic origins through two thousand years of recorded history, has today all the meaning I saw in it when I first wrote it, and more than ever now. When we are witnessing the destruction of so much that is precious and irreplaceable in European civilization, it is not insignificant to learn that this little Provençal town, once situated on a dangerous frontier, was destroyed again and again by barbarians and torn by internecine quarrel, and yet it was rebuilt. It is worth while to remember that nothing material is indestructible, but the spirit in man is.

The whole idea of writing a history of Vence, and the meaning and worth of it, came to me on Armistice Day, in 1929. I was walking the hills outside the little town which looks south upon the Mediterranean and north toward the Alps, with my watch in my hand, waiting for the two minutes of silence. In just a moment, silence would fall upon the Western world, speaking respect for the dead and prayer (how futile we did not know) that war would never come again. Under an iron sky London's traffic would cease its trampling. Paris would pause, in her sad stately boulevards, amidst the fallen leaves, to mourn. Even the whirlpool of New York would stop gyration. Here in the fields outside the ramparts of the little Provençal hill town of Vence, amidst the November roses just coming into bloom and under the olives stretching down to the sea, I listened.

Eleven tolled from the square bell tower of the town, toward which the cannons of the besieger had once been leveled. On a slope below me a young man, stripped to the waist and penny-bronze, began to sharpen his scythe with a fierce and lusty clatter. From above blew down the sound of a woman singing among the vines. The song, with a minor refrain, was old and unhappy. But the singer, her children around her full skirts, was young and ripely contented. Scythe and singer and cricket in the stubble raised a harvest choral in the autumnal air and let the two minutes pass as unheeded as bubbles might slip over the race of an old mill.

It was then that I realized that for Provence the first World War was only one of the wars. That in her sod lie rusting the Templar's two-handed blade and the Arab's scimitar. That Vence, scarred by the sword under her roses, had an epic to tell.

For here, in the land of bold devouring suns, of summers heavy with the scent of Spanish broom on the sheep-nibbled hills, of winters trailing sudden mists, of autumns plump with the fig and winey with the grape, and springs when all the world is checkerboarded with fields of jonquils, violets, and roses—here, between the most storied of all seas and the most storied of all mountains, is a little realm whose capitals are villages, whose palaces are a few ruined watchtowers, and whose story descends straight from the campfires of the cave men. All the life of western Europe through the ages is here, all the mightier movements—Renaissance and Reformation, the spread of Greek culture, the building of the Roman roads, the cataclysm and the fresh blood of the barbarian invasions—expressed in the daily doings and dealings of one village and her neighbors.

True, one might accomplish the same result by writing the history of a Sicilian village or that of any other Mediterranean town. Many such have had more illustrious histories, though that of Vence is not to be despised; after all, it gave four saints and one pope to the world, one of its seigneurs was put in *Paradiso* by Dante, and for almost fifteen hundred years it was a cathedral city. But, as it happens, Vence was and remains the only spot on the soil of Europe for which I could speak. In all other parts of the Continent I have been a visitor, delighted but passing. I lived in Vence, or just outside it, for three years—often too poor to travel any farther than I could walk, or again too content to fly my confines when I might have. I struck personal root in that stony soil, and drew, from its ancient deposits of anguish and hope, the strength to sustain my own.

For my wife and I came to Vence gropingly, like the blind. We had fled the low skies of the north, insupportable to such heavy hearts. We were searching for the light in life, that had all but gone out for us.

That was not the mood in which we had, so short a time before, quit America. We had crossed a wide Atlantic elated with excitement, unafraid to launch the frail bark of our careers with two trusting children aboard, our baby boy and our girl of four happy summers. Two days after our landing, in Paris, she died, of a malady unsuspected and always fatal.

Autumn came. And how sad to an American seem the autumns of northern Europe, when the plane leaves turn from green to sear without glory of color; when the heavy air turns cold and damp without ever having been tingling; when the sky comes low in the short days, and the dampness of the cellars steals up through the walls; when the French go with chrysanthemums to decorate their graves at *Toussaint*, the world without hardly distinguishable from the atmosphere of the tombs. So we took the Blue Train south.

We were searching for sunlight, for the hills where the Royal Provence is ripened in the grape and aged in the vat, for the fields whence came those flowers flown by plane to Paris, in little boxes of split cane— the dark true violets in their heartfelt leaves, the fuming airy golden *mimosa*, the freesias with their goddess breath, the childlike snowdrops and great poppy-flowered anemones, white, and scarlet, and purple.

"Where the lemon blooms,
Where amid dark leaves
The golden orange glows."

We knew so well what we wanted—a house in the country, where in simplicity and quiet we could lay hold on life again. But there were some bitter experiences of house-hunting on the pleasure coast. There were ugly old villas and garish new ones; there were cramped little boxes, and vasty palaces where one seemed to smell still the smoke of the cigars of Russian dukes and Argentinian cattle kings who had inhabited them. There were cities bright with a worldly splendor to which we could not lift our eyes.

And then we found Vence and, just outside it, the villa La Roselière.

No signboard, no agent, told us that it was to let; we merely knew it was our house as soon as we saw it, low and white-walled, with red-tile roof, amid old olives and fields of November roses. I hung back, I remember, fearing disappointment, while my wife ran eagerly up the steps to lift the bronze knocker. I turned to the garden, longing to give her all this. The little plot was edged with clipped rosemary; a thin jet of fountain rose and fell in a stone basin flanked by benches of hewn white stone. The hour was the last of sunlight, the shadows lengthening out. The air was wholly still, but with that edge of chill in it, touched with the dry sweetness of winter *mimosa*, which I was to come to know so well. It was as still as if all this—the flowery terraces, the distant sea, the grapes, the fountain amid the rosemary— were elf gifts that might vanish before I could give them to her. I felt that the light was brief—briefer than anyone knew.

Then I heard her voice, happy and excited, calling me to come and see. For the house *was* to let. Within was a fireplace heaped with great cones from the cluster pines; there was real Provençal furniture, its carven walnut surfaces mounted with silver at the keyholes; there was Provençal pottery on the big old dresser, quaintly patterned wallpaper, and—bless God—no pictures but the window-framed long hills and valleys falling to the bright blue sea.

So began our life there. Those were years so stabbingly felt—so mixed with sorrow for the child we had lost, and rapture in the one we had, and the one we now created—that I cannot write of them. There were hours, too, when my mind was dark with frustration and despair over the failure of my work as a writer. Yet the Midi sun poured into my life—an unrelenting friend. It was impossible not to hope, to believe, to take rapture in the daily rhythm of living, in a place so fair, among a people so cordial and enduring.

How snugly the Vençois lived within the walls of their little town, a pleasant walk of three kilometers from our door! How cheerfully they went afield each morning—for many of the peasants live in the town and go out daily to their little morsels of earth on the mountainsides—their donkeys trotting patiently at their sides. (No farmer there owns a car, for the same reason that I did not; it is quite beyond him in price and upkeep, while the donkey which forages for it-self costs nothing, having been born of its mother be-fore it. And indeed in its asinine way it may love you. A coughing Citroën does not love you. *Eh b'en, aloura!*)

And how sweet was their life—and ours—in the country places where the crocus and ladies'-tresses starred the grass under the olives in autumn, and wild slim hyacinths and little bee-orchis enameled it in spring! It is said that there is not a new flower or bird left on the continent of Europe for the naturalist to discover. And though this is true for European naturalists, it was all as new to me as Botany Bay to Captain Cook. It was all new, and yet all very old —every least flower encrusted with legends and with names in all the languages in Europe, the Provençal closest of all to the classic Latin by which Virgil and Horace called their roses, their laurel bush and myrtle and fig, olive and pine and anemone. And nothing that I had ever heard from the poets of the nightingale prepared me for that incomparable voice which rose, the first night of May, from the moonlit olives. I was never able, when it sang, to go to sleep, but though nodding with weariness I would prop myself on an elbow, drinking in every note until the song would be "buried deep in the next valley glades." I do not deny the force of association: Keats and Matthew Arnold and Swinburne, the nightingale passage in the "Pastoral Symphony," the Greek legends, the sense of olden lovers, all had their effect. But in European Nature nothing is divorced from its associations, for everything has them.

Thus I was led step by step toward an interest, at first casual, then absorbing, in the history of this land and these people. I could step right back into the past by simply walking up St. Raphaël Mountain from my back door, through the olives where the chaffinch sang and the hoopoe flashed, up through the *maquis* suffocating in the fragrance of blossoming broom, till I reached the terraces of the old commune of Malvans, an abandoned and vanished village given over to wild thyme and lavender. Here were the ruins of a Templars' keep, and the Château de Malvans—a gaunt shell of a tower, popularly called Queen Jeanne's, in honor of the woman who set Provence ablaze, in the days of her friends Boccaccio and Petrarch, with her intrigues and love affairs, her wars and her beauty and her wickedness. There was a little chapel up there on a knoll, where once a year, on St. John's or Midsummer's Day, a priest came to say Mass, when peasants and their children and dogs climbed by little goat tracks from all directions to answer the sound of the lonely bell.

> "Poor little place, where its one priest comes
>   On festa-day, if he comes at all,
> To the dozen folk from their scattered homes,
>   Gathered within that precinct small
>   By the dozen ways one roams."

"And all day long a bird sings there,
   And a stray sheep drinks at the pond at times;
The place is silent and aware;
   It has had its scenes, its joys and crimes,
But that is its own affair."

Up there in the hills were cellar holes of old farmhouses; there were the ruins of mills where once the people of Malvans had ground their wheat. No golden corn grows there now; only the sheep crop at the fescue, bleating and shaking their bells in the echoing silence.

If I climbed still higher, I mounted to the great stone plain that rolls away and away till it rises in the barren ridge of the Cheiron Range. From those plains I could see the white-hooded procession of the Alps marching across the sky to the northeast, and they brought the thought of longed-for places—all the rich and carven heart of Central Europe. It seemed very lonely here, by contrast, with only the crested larks, tossed apart by the wind, keeping in touch—mate with mate—by their whistled calls of *whee-wheeyou*. Yet even here the evidence of man, and the past, was about me. There were great circles of erected stones, and stones laid like altar tables across others, and cairns of stone, all bespeaking the prehistory of the stone-worshiping Nerusii. There was one great boulder balanced upon another at which I never ceased to wonder, until a young woman, herding her sheep, gravely informed me that it had been placed there by Roland, who lifted it out of Charlemagne's way as he was journeying by to Rome.

Filled with such immediate impressions, I began secretly to write the Vence history. Rash and ill-equipped as I was, I felt as though I had experienced the landfall of a continent and were setting out to explore it from ocean to ocean, from misty past to illimitable future. The sources I had at my command were what the historian calls secondary—that is, they were not the original documents on which history is based, but accounts synthesized from those documents. I realize very well that to win the respect of historians I ought to have gone back to the primary sources. I ought to have been a trained archivist and archeologist. I ought to have known how to read manuscripts in Latin and medieval French and in Provençal and Italian, and to have spent years over the records of the cathedrals at Vence, Grasse, and Nice, over the archives of Aix-en-Provence, Marseille, and Turin, where beyond a doubt, there are mentions of Vence without number in the acts, deeds, treaties, and other documents of this part of the world. In addition, I ought to have devoted a quarter of a lifetime to research in the Bibliothèque Nationale and the Vatican Library. This done, I should then have spent twenty years digging in the ruins of the castle at La Gaude and the Templars' commandery of St. Martin and in the tower called Queen Jeanne's, as well as in the site of the village of Malvans. I should have delved about the druidical stone circles; I ought literally to have unearthed the remains of Greek and Roman civilization, the Keltic Bronze Age, the Cro-Magnon and Neanderthal Stone Ages. Then, indeed, I might have been fitted, by the standards of scholarship, for the task I undertook.

I ought, in short, to have been not one but several old gentlemen of independent means and a painstaking, cataloguing frame of mind.

If I lacked both the training and the source material of a scholar, I was also both financially and temperamentally unfitted for leisurely research. I was at that moment in life when a man's success or failure is in the balance. So I drove myself industriously every day to my desk and tried to earn ready money in the only way I knew how to attempt—the writing of short stories for American magazines. It was not that I despised that art; I admired it. I simply had no gift for it. And more, there was a definite conflict in my mind.

This was all due to this history on which I was covertly working, with no possible hope that it could be printed, or would sell if it were, or even be read. I judged it as completely off my track. I had to be a modern, didn't I? And write brightly of a bob-haired lovely who said pert things to her college "juvenile" —while all the time, at the back of my mind, I was secretly in love with a certain Aicarde de Castellane who rode over these hills, in the twelfth century, to be the bride of the warlike Seigneur de Villeneuve.

Only at twilight did I release myself from dutiful hacking. Then, when the day's wine was turned to crimson dregs of sunset behind the Estérels' volcanic jagged outlines, when the big blue carpenter bees had left the hedge-flower's lip, and the mistral rose and rattled olives down on the roof, when the candles and the fire of olive logs were lit, when my wife was curled on the hearth, her head against my knee and my hand in her hair, we would look in the flames, sometimes sorrowing together, always in love. And the old loves and the old sorrows of all the thousands of lives that had been before us here would rise up before me, real as my own, asking, I thought, to be voiced.

So presently I would slip off to a small, chill room, empty of all but table and chair, and for an hour I would write on my history of Vence. I remember that I never paused for a word or a conviction. Every moment at that little desk by candlelight was rapture and ease. I failed to understand the contrast between my day of futile, struggling composition, and work on the Vence history, which was as effortless and as much a part of myself as bleeding. I supposed I was riding a hobby; I did not dream that all day I flogged a wooden horse, and only in the dusk, for an hour, did I allow myself to mount a living steed. Not that my work was so good, but that my subject was so great. And in this little book I found what voice I have.

If it was foolhardy of me to attempt to write history without a historian's training, I had one great advantage, not always enjoyed by better historians than I. I was living in the place and among the people of whom I wrote, for to live with the Vençois was to live with their ancestors. They are all but unaffected by the changes wrought by an industrialized world, and they are the direct descendants of the tenants of these houses and fields for ten centuries. The historian of New York cannot point to a house, or a foot of soil, or a single contemporary New Yorker unchanged from Peter Stuyvesant's day. In treating of seventeenth-century Manhattan, he writes of something remote and intangible. But Vence within its walls three hundred years ago was only slightly different from Vence today, whether we are speaking of the streets and houses, or the people who inhabit them.

As the peasants lived by candlelight, so did we, having no electricity. As they warmed themselves at olive and pine fire, we did so. We drank goat's milk, and kept it cool in running spring water outside the kitchen door, having no more refrigerator than anyone else. We had no telephone, either. Whatever these people about us had, we had; what they lacked, we lacked. Probably no woman in Vence has ever had anesthetics at childbirth, and my wife got none when our second son was born. But on her return with the baby in her arms, her neighbors loaded her with roses and gillyflowers, robbed from their destiny at the Grasse perfumeries. And old men stopped her to ask gravely if she had plenty of milk for the little one? If we were outsiders, these good people did not intend us to suffer from it.

Indeed I soon found myself up to my nose in their life. I learned to fear with them the *huissier*, the licensed tyrant who collects bills and keeps every French town in terror. When the local bank failed, I was in the same pickle as my neighbors. Not that I lost money; I mean that the two thousand francs (eighty dollars) which I had borrowed from the lenient banker was now called in by pitiless creditors of the fallen institution. And all around me there was a similar scramble for sums that looked equally mountainous.

I submit that even such small experiences were valuable to the historian of these people, and go some little way to compensate for the advantages of a genuine historian who sits down in an airtight cubbyhole deep in the stacks of a vast library, to write of a people he cannot find from documents only he can read.

What I really wanted to write about was stuff for which there is no documentation. I wanted to tell the story of one old *mas* or farmhouse, with biographies and portraits of its rosy, horny-fingered owners, its olive-skinned fertile women. To chronicle the cult of the *masques*. To write the story of an ell of Provençal hillside earth. For behind the great gorgeous curtain of historical event, broidered with prince and pope, baron and bishop, run the mice of Time, sly, shy, humble-colored, and busied with their own concerns.

The footfalls scurry behind the arras, but the curtain will not lift. So I turned back humbled, as we all must be before humanity, to write the story pictured on the obvious tapestry. Here are the woven figures of Lombard and Gaul and Greek, Saracen, baron and bandit, Caesar and saint, and the dim predecessors of all—the men of the Stone and Iron Ages, whose history was writ only in smoke. Here is depicted in miniature the greater part of the story of the Mediterranean world—its dramas of outward event, dramas of inward idea and ethic. The ramparts of Vence, round which one may stride in fifteen minutes, circumvallate more than an obscure village sunning itself at peace. They inclose, as a living cell incloses the secret of life, a microcosm of the history of Europe. This history was made by men. It is men who must make Europe's future. May they, and we their brothers, take courage from those long gone before!

Table of Contents

Chapter One

THE STONE AGES

FIFTY THOUSAND YEARS BEFORE CHRIST, WHEN THE cave lion was king in the pre-Alps of eastern Provence (where today I sit and write this, looking across the Mediterranean), there was no far-flung glittering shore like that on which the pleasure cities of the Riviera shine, but only a valley plain sloping down to a shrunken salt lake. There great beasts roamed, the lion and the mammoth, the bear and the bison. And one of the beasts was man.

From that time to this, varied waves of humanity have washed across this scene. Flood wrote and ebb erased. But if the whole of the time from that little

1

shambling Neanderthal man were reckoned as one day, from sun to sun, then the written record that is history would be only one hour old.

The piecing-together of those other forty-eight thousand years is beyond the realm of history. It is prehistory. But it is part of this story, the story of man, of *Homo*, upon this little stage that is bounded by the mountains and the sea, by the river Var upon the east and the Loup upon the west. In the cold, wet Mousterian dawn of human times, Neanderthal man slouched across this scene, leaving a few of his primitive stone tools in the earth, and the chars of his campfires. Fire he had, and tools of a sort. Thoughts of a sort he had too, in that thick skull of his, and a little speech. Sometimes, perhaps, he buried his dead, but not often. Sometimes he lived in a cave, yet most of his bones have not been found in caves. He could not stand straight because the structure of his apelike knee joints would not let him. He could not speak plainly, because his chimpanzee jaw did not give enough freedom to his tongue. He could not think clearly, because the lack of frontal development in his skull deprived him of the very centers of conceptual thought and reasoning; the great lobe of his brain was all near the top of the spine, where the senses send their messages. He was an ugly, probably furry brute; he was all that we jokingly picture "the cave man" to have been.

But the true cave man, who triumphed later, was none of these things. He stood erect, as tall as we and sometimes taller, and his knees locked like ours when he drew himself up straight. His chin jutted forward, his brow was strong, his brain capacity the equal of ours. In short, he was *Homo sapiens*—he was ourselves from twenty-five thousand to eighteen thousand years ago. In physical and mental possibilities he differed from us in no essential respect more than we differ from one another today.

We know these things to be true not only in a general way, but specifically for this part of Europe. For the bones of the cave man, of *Homo sapiens* of Aurignacian times (in an interval between the last two advances of the great ice caps), have been found in a state of incomparable preservation very near to Vence. No farther off than at Grimaldi in Italy, only a few feet from the French border.

There are caves here at Vence too. Behind this little villa, behind the town which is the subject of my story, rear great gray shoulders of limestone mountainside, known to the Vençois as the *baous*—an American from the Far West would call them buttes. They are pitted with black spots which are caves, and here have been found, I am told, the bones of cave lion, cave bear, and cave hyena. If these high and lonely caverns have not yet vouchsafed any human skeletons or artifacts, it is, I venture, only from lack of thorough excavation.

3

For not only have caves to the east and to the west of this point been proved once richly inhabited by creatures like ourselves, but all of southern France—overlaid as it is by a sheet of porous, water-soluble limestone—is rich in caves. So it seems to us that *Homo sapiens* in Aurignacian times, the Cro-Magnon man, had the center of his culture here, at least for part of the seven thousand years of his span. Or perhaps France has been more intensively explored than the caves of North and East Africa and of western Asia, where the Cro-Magnon man dwelt too, and fought and mated, hunted and drew pictures, died and was buried. These early men came perhaps from Asia; there are in Europe no skeletons which suggest hybridity between the two species; there is no apparent mingling of their cultures. Instead, *sapiens* supplants *neanderthalensis*, swiftly as geologic time is reckoned. The older species sank into its grave, with crushed skull, its teeth in the Mousterian earth that bore it, the stones and bones and dust and detritus of Aurignacian humanity, for us to find, above it.

Then—having eliminated his only related competitor—man, our kind of man, turned toward the other mammals to contest with them the mastery of the earth.

Up on the *baou* the lonely caverns show like keyholes to the past, the darkness black behind them. Out of that blackness our forebear comes to the mouth of the cave, to challenge the lion's right to it. Henceforth he is to be the hero on this little stage of mine, slain endlessly in inevitable personal defeat, and never defeated. Yet the impartial stars showed him to be a pitiful antagonist to set against the lion. The beast outweighed him many times; its reach and its punch could end the combat in an instant. In cunning the lion is deeper than thought; his instincts and reflexes act for him like coiled springs released. His roar shakes the earth. His eyes can see in the night.

Against him our ancient father stands a soft, naked animal who, fighting on his hind legs, exposes all his most vulnerable organs. He has but those two legs to run upon. His voice frightens nothing bigger than a hare. At night he is all but blind.

Yet those eyes can see what is not visible—the connection between events in the past and others in the future. From this associative memory arises the ability to learn by experience (denied to instinct) and to improve performance. Life does not merely happen to this man. It is remembered, and it is foreseen. And, happening, it makes him weep or laugh. The lion can do neither, nor see how these two uniquely human powers link together the tribe of man by compassion and by criticism.

With such tools of the emotions man is to sculpture out his society. Other marvelous implements he has—his hands, those clever paws that have already learned to make things out of bone and stone and use them for a plotted end. He has a tongue, too, looser in his head than any other primate's, able to speak words for things, to shape from wind in the mouth the stuff that builds higher than stone. His sex life has a pace of its own, slow in growing, so that he has time to learn his complex business of living, and in its maturity not confined to a single brief season of mating. He seeks his woman often, and the consequent sympathy between them binds man's society with ties that he finds sweet and that he tends to draw tighter with those laws called moral.

His young are helpless long, and the need to care for them cements his society with further strength, and so does the long care of the old. Those few other animals that reach old age cannot use it when they do. But the Old Man and, sometimes, the Old Woman have ever been the natural guardians of human tradition. The tongue, the hands, preserve and pass on man's accumulating knowledge. Every litter that the lion bears up there in the unlit cave must begin all over. But with every generation *Homo sapiens* becomes a little richer. Out of his cumulative tradition will emerge the idea, the fact, of tribe, ancestors, descendants, nation, party, sect. Out of the black cave mouth in the *baou* have flowed the springs of human possibility which account for the little town sunning itself today at the *baou*'s foot.

If you would see this man who made us what we are today, if you would look him in the eye and find him brother, go to the Barma Grande, the Great Cave, under the Rochers Rouges beneath the hamlet of Grimaldi just beyond Menton. The caves today are at the very edge of the sea, under steep red cliffs, and to enter them is to step back two hundred centuries and more. The swallows dart ahead of you into the cave, as if to warn the man who lies there—just as he was found, but now under glass—a mighty hunter, his deep eye sockets staring into time, his empty skull echoing with the sob of the sea on the rocks.

Here in the Red Rocks, there have been found fifteen complete human skeletons of the Old Stone Age. The burials occur at various levels down to twenty-five feet, and there may have been a lapse of thousands of years between some of them. But one and all they whisper of the afterlife. These bodies were not left to rot where they fell, but carefully interred here in prepared trenches filled in by a red earth brought, it would seem, for this purpose. The hematite of it has deeply imbued their very bones. Ancient burial in red earth has been found widely elsewhere in Europe, so that we guess it to have had a deep significance, and, guided by the customs of some of today's primitive peoples, we can believe that the color symbolized the blood of life.

The dead thus laid to rest might live again, in some

shadowy primordial other world. The hope is proved by the long hunting knife that the dead cave man carried to his grave, in his left hand, holding the arm flexed as if to strike. Thus, risen from the dead, he could defend himself, and slay the game, the reindeer and horses, the wild sheep and goats and cattle with which, surely, heaven must be populated. Even the children committed to that fearful journey into eternity are not sent forth quite defenseless; we find them provided with little weapons of their own, chips of flint, and with the shells that may have been their playthings. One man grips not a knife but a gypsum crystal—a Stone Age diamond. Was this some man of wealth, not of war, who expects to take it with him and to dazzle or buy off the spirits he will meet? Indeed, all the burials but one are accompanied by possessions of the deceased—necklaces and crowns and anklets and garters made of pierced sea shells, canine teeth of the reindeer, and salmon vertebrae. And some were found to have left the world as they came into it—buried in the fetal position, as if old Mother Earth would bring them forth again at some appointed day of resurrection.

So we know that the cave man was deeply concerned with life after death, for to have evolved so much ritual as even the fragments left to us by time, he must have thought much upon it. It has been said that religion was born of that concern. It is born, too, like man himself, of woman. In the Grimaldi caves, beside innumerable knives and spearheads and scrapers and axes of stone and ivory—enough, indeed, to fill a small museum—there have been found six statuettes and one sculptured head, of human derivation. All but one are female (and this represents the same proportion of females to males as is found among the statuettes of the Aurignacian culture everywhere). Archeologists assert that these female statuettes of the cave man may represent goddesses. For what is a goddess, after all, but woman seen through the eyes of man obsessed with her?

Up to two centuries ago, it is said, there existed at Nice a female statuette, whose darkened antiquity no one pretended to guess, which had been preserved, perhaps from the Old Stone Age itself, with utmost veneration. It was called *la dona mau fauchia*, "the badly made lady," and it was believed to possess such magical and propitiatory powers that in times of plague or of siege or famine it was often paraded through the streets in the sincere belief that it would ward off evil.

Of the old cave man's obsession with woman there is no doubt; most of the statuettes from the Barma Grande, like those found elsewhere, exaggerate the femaleness of the subject; breasts, hips, buttocks, loins, thighs, and belly are emphasized to the neglect of features and even arms. Some of the figures seem to represent pregnancy. You can hardly escape the conclusion that here is a tribute from awed man to the mystery and miracle of fertility which still fascinate him here in Vence as elsewhere all over the world. Here is worship of woman the creator and renewer of life, "death's sleepless foe, from age to age." It is not too much to say that the adoration of the great Mother Goddess, who has had so many incarnations, began here in Cro-Magnon times. Thousands of years later we find it still glowing, celebrated—as the lettering on a Roman stone found in the market place of Vence tells us—under the guise of the Idaean Mother. And it is carried on today, a cult unbroken here since the dawn of man, in the offices of Our Lady, to the tune of *Ave Maria*'s echoing down through two thousand years.

Woman he loved, that tall hunter of the caves, and the magic, the luck, the desperate necessities of the chase. How he would laugh, scorn deep in his bearded lips, to see the peasant creeping through his plot of broad beans to blow the head off a sparrow with a blunderbuss, or take the linnet from the limed twig! The cave man, on these same *baous*, surrounded the mighty mammoth and drove it over the cliff; he caught the fleeing reindeer, and took the wild bull by the horns and felled it. Much of his religion seems to have centered about the magic of the chase, and in its service the masked sorcerer capered—just as we find him doing still in the cave paintings, as among primitive peoples today—in the skins of the animals so venerated and so fiercely desired.

This hunter caught even fish with a spear, or by hand; he had no nets, no fishhooks. He had no domestic animals, no plows, no crops or fields, no bow and arrow, no shield, no cloth, no tents, no pottery or basketry. These things are coming. They are evolved through the ages by the men of the New Stone Age which followed, men of the great and gifted Mediterranean race, the actual ancestors of much of the population of southern Europe and western Asia today. To this sea beside which they dwelt they have, by their accomplishments, left the title of civilization's cradle.

This classic sea, laughing distantly beyond my window, is not timeless like the cold primordial oceans. It is their blue-eyed daughter. There was only a shrunken lake here, while the last of the great ice sheets crushingly overlay Europe, sent a chilling breath far to the south, thrust an arctic tundra vegetation into these hills. But after long ages, the ice began to melt, and that vast quantity of water, so long locked up in glaciers a mile high, returned now to the ocean, so that all over the world the sea-level must gradually have risen. Thus the waves of the Atlantic came to beat on the great earth-gate at Gibraltar, and presently they had plowed clear a channel. Then they poured down into the basin of that old lake known to

11

the Cro-Magnon man, and began to fill it up, as a bowl is filled from a pitcher. Higher and higher rose the water level, drowning the coastal plain, covering, no doubt, innumerable dwelling-places of the Old Stone Age man. Not till the level of the outside ocean was reached did the salty flow cease. At approximately the present shore line of the Mediterranean the waves came at last to beat right at the foot of these Maritime Alps along the Riviera.

Tideless, with numberless harbors and exempt from hurricanes and cyclones, this greatest landlocked sea in the world is the perfect medium for commerce and travel. Once man had invented boats, the Mediterranean drew peoples together more than it separated them. So they found themselves importing and exporting their several languages, alphabets, religions, philosophies, mathematics, astronomy, sculpture, painting, their seeds and fruits and flowers, their music and legend. The Mediterranean is like a stirring pot into which all that is thrown will be circulated and will impart its flavor to mingle with other flavors, and nothing can leak away and be lost to the rich brew, for mountains wall it in everywhere. Many people have sought or fought their way to its shores. Few have ever voluntarily left its genial confines. If old Mother Europe has a womb, it must be the Mediterranean.

For here was born the Mediterranean man, the New Stone Age man who, if he is not the direct descendant of the Cro-Magnon, is certainly his cultural heir. They were a wiry, short-statured, longheaded, olive-skinned, brunet people, from whose rich imaginations has sprung full half the art and science and religion of the Western world, and whose blood still runs warm in it.

In many ways the New Stone Age men remembered their cave heritage. They still sometimes buried their dead in caves, after they no longer occupied them, and they built stone barrows to house the departed. Even today the proper Provençal grave is not a pit in the earth but a little stone house. There are stranger dwelling-places for the dead in this region; almost anywhere hereabout you may encounter a rude stone pile or *pilon*, meaningless to the foreigner but not to the native, who will tell you it marks the spot where a woman met a violent death at the hands of werewolves or those evil spirits called *masques*. It is unlucky for the passer-by not to add a stone. One of the biggest of these *pilons*, near Caussols, still bears on my maps the name of *clapier dè frêmo muorto*—"barrow of the dead woman."

This sense of the spirit in the stone is a bequest straight from the Vençois's New Stone Age ancestor. That early Mediterranean man found in stones a focus for his religious thought. He carved them, often in the semblance of a woman; he ascribed to them the power of fertility. Still in Provence the peasant will

13

place stones in his trees to make them bear fruit. His ancient forebear erected stones in regular rows or in great circles, always on level ground, and several such are still to be found in the neighborhood of Vence. One occurs on the Baou des Pénitents Blancs, near St. Jeannet, and I have discovered a small one in the abandoned commune of Malvans, right up above my villa. On the rock-strewn plateau of Caussols is a great stone circle called by the peasants of today *les murassos*, "the walls." When the Romans came to this country, they considered all such circles to be ancient fortified camps, and called them so, *oppida*. Yet actually they were the crude forerunner of the church.

In the religions of the Mediterranean's people there is a strong continuity. Lost in time is the beginning of belief in a great Mother Goddess, queen of heaven, incarnation of fertility, mistress of crops. Many are the names under which she has been worshiped— Isis, Astarte, Demeter, Ceres, Cybele, Flora, Persephone, Spica, Anaitas, Balaath. She is the Corn Mother, and her gift to humanity is the wheat spike. Mediterranean man found it, an unpromising little wild grass, and bred it, in prehistoric times, into the heavy-headed, sweet-kerneled cereal that makes the French peasant's long loaf today. The Neolithic man discovered winter wheat to be his ideal crop. He sowed it in autumn just before the rains came to sprout it, then reaped it in spring or summer. At sow-

ing and at reaping he established festivals and rites
that we inherit as Easter, May Day, Midsummer, and
Halloween.

The longer one lives here the more one becomes
aware that the Mediterranean man of today has not
forgotten his New Stone Age past, when sun and
fire were worshiped as well as stone and corn. Last
June my birthday was made memorable to me by the
sight of fires that blazed at every farm or *mas;* far
down the slopes toward the sea I could behold their
glow, and up on the terraces above. For Midsummer's
Day is still honored as it was when fires were lit
thousands of years ago in honor of Belen, the sun-god
whose longest reign comes at the summer solstice,
when the night is warm and brief. Because St. John's
Feast falls upon that day, they are called, these bonfires, the St. John's fires, and time was when the children of Provence went about begging fuel of everyone to start them, and woe to him so ungenerous that
he gave none. Youths and maidens jumped over the
blaze hand in hand, repeating the incantation:
"Wheat, grow as high as we can jump," or "Flax,
grow this high."

In Neolithic times, as now, incense was flung upon
such fires, and in the flames died witches and disease
and all the year's sins. No frankincense and myrrh
have the Vençois, as had the eastern Mediterraneans,
but there is a great wealth of aromatic herbs in the

15

native flora. One, an *Artemisia*, that they fling upon the flames for its pungent odor and magical properties is still known by the significant name of *herbe de feu*, or "crown-of-St. John." To drive cattle through the smoke of St. John's fires, so I am told by the good peasant woman who comes every day to scrub and sweep for us, is to protect them from disease. And she informs me that once a year the cows are blessed with hellebore, to drive away evil spirits.

Far back in time the New Stone Age man began the domestication of animals, first the dog, then cattle, as is proved from a very ancient cliff painting formerly to be seen near Ventimiglia which showed men plowing with teams of yoked oxen. It is, historically, a great moment when he first thrusts the plow into the virgin sod, and in the furrow flings the seed, wheat, perhaps, or flax. For flax was Mediterranean man's first fiber, and linen his first raiment after skins. Slowly the Mediterranean woman learned her cleverest skill—to spin, and weave upon the loom.

Sowing crops and tending herds stabilized society. They put an end to the hunter's roaming life. Land as property must now have become a settled concept. Changes were coming over the landscape, too. The forests of oak and hornbeam began to fall, to make room for cultivated fields gold with wheat and blue with flax flowers. Grazing by sheep would destroy the forest and spread the grass. Grazing by goats—the curse of all the Mediterranean lands—destroyed even the grass, till the white bones of the limestone mountains showed as they still do. After the goats could come only the fierce and aromatic *maquis*, that intricate thorny scrub.

So for thousands of years there dwelt here a Neolithic people called the Ligurians, while more gifted Mediterranean peoples were founding the civilizations we know as Egyptian, Etruscan, and Cretan.

Then, about 3000 B.C., at the beginning of the Bronze Age, a new people appeared, a race whose culture centered around the life and death of the warrior. These warrior people pushed far south, into India, Greece, Italy, and France. By the time history begins to dawn, the Romans had a name for them, or at least for the branch of them that they knew best where they had settled in northern Italy. They called them the Gauls, and they described them as a long-boned, gray-eyed people.

Hereabout the Ligurians and the Gauls or Kelts mingled their blood. They made a mixed strain of blonds and brunets, of long heads and round heads, of tall and short, and all combinations intermediate. So was welded the Kelto-Ligurian of the local tribe of the Nerusii, and this commingled people were the direct ancestors, in part, of the living Vençois to whose blood have been added Roman and Frank, Ostragoth and Burgundian.

17

Thus dim in the smoke of Neolithic fires lie the foundations of my immortal village. No one could say now what the Kelto-Ligurians called their town; the Romans translated it as Vintium, which altered through Vintia, Vencia, Vensa, to Vence. But it is not impossible to guess what Vence looked like when it was the capital of the Nerusii. Its houses were crude, low, of clay, perhaps, with doors of woven reeds and wattled roofs pierced with a chimney hole. Everywhere the blue smoke twirls up against the face of the *baous* looking down upon this vigorous people. The warriors swagger about, in wool or linen or the skins of wolf and goat. It is the women who are working, spinning, grinding meal, turning the venison or pig on the spit. In the roadways of this wild but tranquil settlement lumber a few two-wheeled carts, and, where the huts end and the fields begin, a horse is drawing a rough plow. All about are swarms of sturdy, naked children begging for food, playing at work, or sleeping casually as puppies. Not far off, right on the same hill in fact, are the tombs of these people's ancestors. It is said by archeologists that that cemetery was in the Place Godeau, and that every ounce of dust in that ground, stirred today by boys at their scuffling play, represents the living flesh of the forgotten forefathers of the village.

Into this camp come suddenly strange men— Phoenician traders, sea-going Semites, who have found their way to the western Mediterranean, trading, buying, selling, bargaining with their long soft brown hands. What they have to show amazes the Nerusii. There are beads and glassware, tinware from the mines of Britain, iron pots, mirrors of polished bronze, fabrics of cloth dyed with gorgeous colors. There are knives, swords, and axes of iron. The age of iron has met the dying age of stone and bronze, and a rich, seductive civilization tempts the hardy Nerusii. The bargaining is sharp; it grows angry. Suddenly the Nerusii seize some of the coveted goods. Swords are lifted on each side. The glassware is broken, the fabrics are torn, in the struggle. The Phoenicians, outnumbered and robbed, indemnify themselves by seizing a dozen boys and girls to be sold as slaves in some far-off port.

The isolation of the Nerusii is over. More and more often strangers will come, bringing new temptations, new gods, new fruits, new languages. The name of the Nerusii will be recorded in the annals of these strangers. Written history has begun. The world is to hear of Vence.

Chapter Two

THE CLASSIC AGE

IT WAS THE PHOCAEAN GREEKS WHO BROUGHT THE classic touch to Provence. These seem to have been a peaceful, ingratiating, and industrious people who came from the town and district of Phocaea, northernmost of the Ionian cities on the Asiatic shore of the Aegean Sea. Their ancient settlement is still known as the Turkish town of Fokia, close to the city of Smyrna famous for its fine figs. Phocaea had a fine harbor and a resourceful hinterland, and was hence led naturally to sea commerce, exporting the materials of a rich civilization. For inland lay the kingdom of Lydia, whose king, Croesus, has become a byword for wealth. More, the star of Persia was rushing west-ward, carrying with it the religions, the manufac-tories, the science, the wealth, and the seductions of all the ancient civilizations to which it had fallen heir. So the Phocaean Greeks had much to import and buy, and to export and sell again. They had the sailors and the ships; all they needed was the markets.

In the eastern Mediterranean these were closed to them. The Phoenician cities of Tyre and Sidon had all but a monopoly of the carrying trade there, and the rich old civilizations of the Near East produced the very things the Phocaeans had to sell. So the Phocae-ans turned to the western Mediterranean, and pushed out with extreme boldness, considering their frail craft and the unknown seas and hostile tribes they had to encounter. Although the Sicilian and Italian Greeks were far nearer to these new markets, the Phocaeans showed much greater business enterprise and exploratory genius. Already by 600 B.C. they had founded their greatest colony of Massilia, the modern Marseille. Antipolis, which we call Antibes, had been founded by 340 B.C., and perhaps about the same time was built the city of Nikaia, or Nice, that glittering center of which Vence is a shy country cousin.

So they must have come climbing up into our hills, traders in the rich stuffs of the East who bought—it is not quite clear just what. Perhaps grain, perhaps furs, wool, timber, or slaves. Some sort of raw material they must have got here, for the Kelto-Ligurians could have had little else to sell to more civilized people. In this part of Provence the Greeks must have felt themselves at home. Here they found again the flashing sea, the marvelous Mediterranean sky, the mountains descending grandly to the water, now barely clad with thyme, now forested with the myrtle and laurel sacred to them, and the ilex oak that Homer sings of. Add but the obedient olive tree, the bleating flocks, the wine presses, the shepherd's pipe, the white Ionic column, and Gaul was become another Greece, like Greece before the Fall, before the civil wars, before the sins and sorrows and conscious splendors of a world grown wise and wicked—halfway, in short, between Homer and Pericles.

There is no evidence that the Greeks ever actually settled in Vence. But there is every reason to think that the Nerusii were familiar with Greek traders and the stuff they sold. And it is highly likely that to the Greeks the Vençois of today owe the olive, the fig, the cypress, the chestnut, the caper, and perhaps the hyacinth, oleander, acanthus, and pomegranate, as well as the vine of the grape.

The Provençal could hardly imagine life without his good companions, the fig, the vine, and the olive. Nor can we, his foreign guests, imagine the landscape without them. The olive is the chief of these, emblem of peace and prosperity, the tree whose leaves were kind to Christ at Gethsemane. Round its simple economy the peasant of Vence built his life, slowly but increasingly abandoning first flax, then wheat inherited from a prehistoric past, and producing instead an oil crop, an ideal stuff of export, capable of intensive culture, furnishing a living for twenty families where, perhaps, only one could live by wheat-farming or grazing.

The silvery dome of the olive tree is the first thing that the visitor from the north sees when he raises the curtain of his berth on the Blue Train, down from Paris, and looks out on the flashing sea and the white-boned hills. So it becomes his first love, this tree that climbs the terraces in row on row, that leans across every path from the bank above, that shades the door of the wayside chapel, and stands, centuries after the walls have vanished, around old cellar holes and ruined mills, reminder of the briefness of the life of man, its master. Later one may become beguiled by other trees—the haughty palms of which one again grows tired, the dramatic cypresses which finally come to look like so many exclamation points in the poetry of the landscape, and the orange, golden among its glittering leaves.

But in the end you come back to your first love, the olive, true symbol of this woman-land of Provence with its fair face and warm fertility, its swarming children, its graces and dancing, its music and flowers. For the olive is the most domesticated, the least wild of trees. Nor can I think of another that so bespeaks history. Infinitely slow of growth, it never grows straight; it leans and twists; it is eccentric and individualized, as if the centuries had worked upon it. As indeed they have; some of the olive groves of the Riviera are said to go back at least to Roman times, almost two thousand years. And they look it, rivaled in bulk and grandeur and age only by the chestnuts.

The harvest of grapes in Provence is drunken with sunshine; the harvest of flowers for the perfume trade is fragrant and joyous. But the olives are picked in winter, when the bright air is chill and the fingers of the peasant children are red with cold as they creep along the ground to gather up the little black fruits that have been beaten from the trees. The European robin, the redbreast, sings then his sad winter song; in the clear green-gold of sunset the silvery trees turn dark. And to watch the little figures beneath them, on some hill across a stream murmuring icily, is to look at a little picture that seems, even as you gaze, to become a memory of something long ago and very far off.

To the Greeks, some say, we owe the Battle of Flowers (introduced by them, perhaps in connection with the rites of Demeter or Adonis, or the worship of Persephone, at Marseille), carried on by the Romans and never abandoned. The foreigner who has seen only the Battle of Flowers at Nice can have no conception of the spontaneity, the gaiety and charm of the festival as practiced at Vence. Instead of a lackadaisical procession of the floats of wealthy merchants and the carriages of visitors who wish to appear in the public eye, the flower battle of Vence is a naïve fete, appropriately attended by the Arlesian dancers in their old Provençal costumes, who combine some of the circular figures of Greek choral dancing with the drum and fife of Moorish original. Into the Place du Grand Jardin swings the band of the Chasseurs Alpins from the barracks at Grasse, their brasses glittering and blaring. Windows are flung up, and children troop out, the boys in white with red sashes, the girls in all the old costumes, the striped skirts and lace caps and great cartwheel black straw hats worn on the head or down the back. And now at last come the carts, two-wheeled and four-wheeled, drawn by little donkeys with sprigs of violets and freesias in their ears, and hoofs gilded for the occasion. Everywhere dart the vendors of nosegays, and from the laughing spectators to the proud peasants in their carts flies back and forth a barrage of roses and violets, mignonette and freesia, hyacinths and jonquils, narcissus and daffodils, gillyflowers and orange blossoms. After the battle comes the gay ceremony of crowning the chosen Queen of Love and Beauty. And

25

so for a day, while the fountains tinkle, and the gray mists wreath the *baous* and the sea wind and sunshine commingle all the odors of salt and pine and orange and violet, Vence revives again the spirit of a sinless age.

In other ways too, perhaps, she remembers unconsciously the Hellenic springs of our civilization. For with the Grecian flocks came the worship of Pan, the shepherd's divinity, he of the cloven hoof and shaggy thighs, the crumpled horn and pointed ears. All through the Middle Ages the legend of the Golden Goat, the *chèvre d'or*, was to haunt Provence. Indeed, he never left Provence, though it is becoming harder and harder, for people who have grown too wise, to perceive him. However, sometimes the crescent of his horns may be seen rising at nightfall above the hills, and he dances on Christmas Eve and St. John's Day. If you find one of his hairs upon a mountain rock, you must put it in a bag and wear it around your neck.

Though the Greeks here came for peaceful penetration, the Nerusii of Vence, like the coastal tribes near Marseille, Antibes, and Nice, gave them a hostile reception. There were numberless border skirmishes between the Greeks and Ligurians. In the year 155 B.C. the Phocaean colonists sent to the Roman senate to ask help against the barbarians who were laying siege to Nice, Antibes, and Marseille. The Greek cities deserved well of Rome, having opposed

26

the passage of Hannibal through Gaul, and the Romans sympathized with their efforts to establish civilization on a barbaric coast. So they sent an unarmed ambassador to Aegytna (modern Cannes). As soon as the boat touched shore, the Ligurians rushed down and attacked it.

The angered senate at Rome then dispatched the consul Quintus Opimius, who arrived at Aegytna and burned it. Then, marching inland in order to draw the Ligurians away from beleaguered Nikaia and Antipolis, he seems to have struck out straight toward Vence. Somewhere on the banks of the river Loup, probably not more than four kilometers from Vence, the Ligurians came up with him. In two successive engagements Rome triumphed decisively. This is the first appearance of Roman troops upon our little stage. Again and again it will shake to their heavy tramp, until at last they come to fill it, like a chorus all through an act that is to last almost five hundred years.

All southern Gaul had presently for its governor a young officer named Gaius Julius Caesar. Still the region of Vence was probably in only nominal subjection to Rome until the reign of the first emperor, Augustus. In the year 14 B.C. he turned his attention to the independent tribes of the western and maritime Alps. Eleven years earlier he had begun what, in soldier talk, is called a mopping-up process, on

Rome's northern frontiers. The Nerusii were among the last tribes to succumb. But, according to some accounts, two Roman armies are converging on them. One has just conquered the people in the valley of the Esteron, and now the Roman eagles come glittering over the Cheiron Range, down the sloping stone plains to the top of the *baous*. The other Roman force, which has just been subjecting the tribes in the hills north of Nice, crosses the Var and advances from the east. Thus are the Nerusii caught and conquered. Then the Roman chariot wheels roll on toward Grasse and Castellane, methodically crushing out opposition in every last corner.

This is the last we ever hear of the Nerusii, or almost the last. Their name appears as the forty-second on a list of forty-five tribes that was engraved upon the Trophy of Augustus, the great monument of victory which was raised in Caesar's honor at La Turbie, upon a high cliff above the Mediterranean and the modern city of Monte Carlo. This pompous structure, now a haughty ruin but once faced with marble and glittering with gold ornaments, must have been visible far out at sea. Erected on that part of the coast longest considered impassable to Roman might, it was meant to impress the world and the infinite future with the magnificence of Augustus and the empire, and to remind the hill tribes forever of their defeat.

How Roman civilization came to Vence there is no

record. By a common custom the lands of the conquered were in those days often given to the Roman
veterans, their former owners being either slain or
sold into slavery. If the veteran did not already have
a family, he quite commonly took a woman of the
conquered race to wife. On this Rome looked with
favor; it Romanized the next generation with marked
success. The son, taught to be proud of his Roman
blood, might drive his plow through the skull of his
Ligurian grandsire and be none the wiser or sadder.

So Roman Gaul is coming to birth. For once having
embraced the Roman, Provence accepted him with in-
creasing ardor, and remained true to Rome in all the
long struggles of the empire. Many of Rome's finest
monuments are found in western Provence, at
Nîmes, Arles, and Avignon, at Fréjus and in the
ruins of the theater at Cimiez above Nice. Temples,
aqueducts, roads, baths, bridges, portrait busts—all
that for which the Roman had an especial genius was
lavished upon Provence. Here the Roman found a
purer Rome than the parent-city, a happier Rome,
sunnier, more spacious, more peaceful and fertile. A
Rome without the mobs, without the imperial guards,
the inbred families, the mad emperors of the capital.
The Gallo-Roman, said Cicero, had two citizenships,
that of Rome and that of his homeland.

The archeologist Edmond Blanc has thoroughly in-
vestigated the Roman remains and inscriptions of

Vence. For votive monuments still speak to us, from mute fragments, of religious festivals and special sacrifices. One gives thanks for a successful harvest— gratitude to Cybele, goddess of the grain—while another shows that the worship of Mars was practiced here. The town's chief historian, the Abbé Tisserand, believes he can even give, from fragments of engraved stone, the names of some of the principal Roman resident families, such as Talatorius, Malamater, and Mars. Each day in the Place Antony Mars, I stop for a loaf of bread. Old Madame Malamaire hands me roses over the fence dividing her property from mine. Poring over the doings of councilmen in the history of medieval Vence, how often I have met the name of Taladoyre!

The most famous of all the Vence inscriptions, because the most legible, is that which relates that: "To the Idaean[1] Mother Cybele, Valeria Marciana, Valeria Carmosine and Cassius Paternus the priest have celebrated a *taurobolium* at their own expense." So once in the market place of Vence was performed the hideous ceremony of the bull. In the *taurobolium*, the priest descended into a pit, stabbed a sacrificial bull laid over the opening, and let the blood gush over him. When he arose, dripping, his person and even his gory garments were sacred in the eyes of Cybele's worshipers.

[1] Cybele, goddess of the grain, was supposed to have a favorite residence on Mount Ida, behind Troy—hence "the Idaean Mother."

The one fragment of Rome which still stands is the pillar in the center of the Place Godeau. Vence is proud of this, its most ancient monument, and likes to call it "the mystery stone." To make a mystery of it, some have called it a Kelto-Ligurian object of stone worship, others a Greek boundary stone. But who can think the Neolithic people capable of cutting so pure a shaft? And if the Greeks had a boundary here, why is no more trace of it found? No, this, I think, is a last sentinel of Rome, proudly erect still. It is of blue porphyry, such as may be quarried in the volcanic Estérels; without its base, its stands about ten feet tall, delicately tapered, and capped with a simple capital. The inscription on the pedestal—if the pedestal belongs with the column—proclaims that it is a gift from Massilia (Marseille) to the city of Vintium. The dim words are in Latin, a tongue certainly not understood here before 100 B.C., and probably not the common language of Marseille or Vence until a century later. Like many another survival of the pagan age, this perdurable monolith has been adopted by the wise old Church, and topped triumphantly with a cross.

From the nature of the Roman inscriptions found around Vence, it seems certain that the town must have had a forum, temples, villas, aqueducts, and, consequently, a whole official body of decurions, decemvirs, priests, and magistrates. Looking back through time, one sees shafts of white marble, topped by gilded capitals, streets lively with throngs of roundheaded, white togaed men and stout ladies in voluminous draperies; one pictures the centurion pacing his rounds with his spear, the rich gentleman's litter, the arriving of messengers covered with the dust of the post road, the market full of hides and cloths and kids and cattle, with a sprinkling, perhaps, of mountain children dismally awaiting sale. It is easy to imagine Vence as a model little provincial sub-capital, but it may just as likely have been one of those muddy, impoverished military posts in the hill district to which the Roman prayed his gods the government would not send him.

This much is certain—that Vence lay upon the Via Julia. The Julian Road ran from La Turbie of the victory monument to Grasse or near it, and beyond, through the Estérel Mountains, toward western Provincia. Monsieur Blanc has discovered for us that this artery of Rome's greatness was three and a half meters wide, and built of enormous blocks of quarried stone a yard square, laid upon a rubble foundation to a depth of fifteen inches. From St. Jeannet, the Via Julia ran to Vintium or Vence, and then through the oak woods of La Conque and down into the valley of the Malvans below my villa. It is little more than a deep lane now, but still in use by peasants' carts, school children, and Sunday-evening lovers, who follow it past the ruined chapel of Bon Voyage, as it stumbles down over bedrock with shell fossils still embedded in it. Then it crosses on a masonry bridge—beneath which primroses lie gold in spring—and mounts up through the quarter of La Sine. That is where my good peasant woman Thérèse lives, she who keeps the red-tile floors of the villa bright and beats our clothes white with a paddle in cold running spring water. Her dwelling-place is the ruin of a fine old Provençal *mas* of the early eighteenth century. Neighbor to this, Monsieur Blanc unearthed the vestiges of a Roman villa. Home is as old here as the heart of man.

Where the old Via Julia climbs up above the present Grasse road, just beyond my villa, I regularly walk its stony way, meeting only a goat or a child, until it descends on what is now Tourrettes. Here the legions clanked, their armor glittering in the summer sunlight. Here the lady was borne in her litter. Then as now the little donkey plodded under sacks of olives, the brown-skinned country children ran after their father's cart, stopping to pluck the wayside blackberries, or the frail rock-rose that perished in their hands.

The road from Rome brought Provence the cherry and almond, the mulberry, quince, and peach. Every good Roman villa had a garden, and Roman gravestones of Provence pay tribute to forgotten gardeners pictured with their pruning knives and spades. Poppies and narcissus, violets and lilies, were loved. But the rose was the favorite of all—that which the ancients called the rose of Paestum, brought to Italy by the Sybarites from Greece, which in turn had borrowed it from Persia, its native home. On this exquisitely fragrant flower, already known in Roman times in double form and many shades, Nero spent fantastic sums for a single festival; today it is known as the Provence rose, or *rose de mai*, and the peasants grow it for the sake of its petals whence are expressed the reluctant drops of attar. The love of flowers was one of the tenderest sides of the Roman, who had so much about him that was purely practical and no little sheerly brutal. One stone, found in Provence, shows a Gallo-Roman woman behind a counter, holding a wreath, and bears the advertisement: *Garlands for lovers only*.

From the gravestones of the Gallo-Romans found all over Provence can be pieced together much of the life and thought of the man of Vintium. The stones speak of bakers and barbers, of children and pets, of wineshops and inns, of sheep-shearing and wine-pressing, of music on the seven-tubed pipe, of the changing styles in which ladies do their hair. And over and over they speak to us of grief, not only the formalized mourning which is chiefly a tribute to the importance of the surviving family, but in the genuine accents of bereavement. A young mother, a kind protecting husband, a pretty child, each is laid in the tomb with a voiced agony that can still be felt. Cumulatively, these stones remind us how much more of humanity is under the sod than above it. And we feel too how steeped in pagan philosophy were these lives cut off so long ago. As there is implied in the inscriptions no consciousness of sin and no expectation of a Judgment Day, so there is no suggestion of future bliss or reunion. Again and again the Gallo-Roman funerary epitaphs begin: "Stay thy footsteps, passing stranger, and read of one beloved who in life. . . . ." In life, in Roman Vintium, long ago, where the centuries passed with a slow proud tread of sandaled feet. Where the will of some new Caesar is proclaimed in the square; where children are born and begin to wail, folk are married and begin to grumble, and men grow old, feeling both hope and fear that they may die.

CHRONOLOGY FOR CHAPTER TWO

FROM THE FOUNDING OF THE ROMAN EMPIRE
TO THE LAST PAGAN EMPEROR

27 B.C. Octavianus, Caesar Augustus
14 A.D. Tiberius
37   Gaius Caesar, nicknamed "Caligula"
41   Claudius
54   Nero
69   Vespasian
79   Titus

81 A.D.	Domitian
96	Nerva
98	Trajan
117	Hadrian
138	Antoninus Pius
161	Marcus Aurelius
180	Commodus
193	Septimus Severus
211	Caracalla
217	Macrinus
218	Elagabalus
222	Severus Alexander
235	Period of the "phantom emperors" begins. Among them may be mentioned the following, whose names appear on tablets found around Vence:
238	Gordonianus III
244	Julius Philippus
249	Decius
253	Valerianus
276	Probus
285	Valerius Maximus
322	Constantine
353	Constantius
361	Julian the Apostate

Chapter Three

THE DARK AGES

So THROUGH ITS LONG GOLDEN AUTUMN THE ROMAN world stood like a forest hung with motionless, splendid foliage. But it was a deceptive calm, and the leaves at last must fall before the northern wind. The time was at hand when the barbarians could no longer be staved off. And added to the enemy without there was the enemy inside the lines, the Christian, a fellow—as the pagan Roman saw him—who denied that Caesar was the supreme king, who favored pacifism and the communism of property, who wanted a prohibition on almost everything and a censorship on the rest, a fanatic who smashed up art treasures and proclaimed the imminent end of the world.

37

The stories of the saints and the barbarians, as far as Vence is concerned, go hand in hand and must be told together, for as fast as the barbarians were gentled by the Church, the Church took on barbarian vigor, and changed from the chiton of Greek speculation to the crude, splendid colors of medieval robes. At first the Christian theology had seemed inextricably mired in the bloodless metaphysics of the Greeks. Dissensions of Christology were once capable of setting city against city, and even in Provence there flourished fantastic heresies.

The coming of Christianity to Vence is entirely legendary. St. Trophimus of Arles is traditionally stated to have brought the Word to Vence. The tales of saints and martyrdoms in this part of Provence are local miracle myths that bear a monotonous and even suspicious resemblance to each other and to other martyrdom miracles in Italy, Greece, Syria, and Egypt—lions that would not eat the Christians fed to them, martyr fires that would not burn, severed heads that floated down streams, between blue flames.

More convincing is that citizen Nazarius of Nice who took a hammer to the statue of Venus in the glades of Arluc, at the mouth of the Siagne, and exorcised from the delicious groves of parasol pine a magician named Cloaster. Cloaster was compelled to pull down the high tufted woods; Venus was driven forth; where she had been worshiped a nunnery would rise. In Nazarius some people see a typical early Christian, afraid of art, afraid of sex, afraid of Nature, which he endowed with evil magic, and magnificently unafraid of all the legions of Caesar.

Even the well-known date of A.D. 363, when a St. Audinus is claimed by some to be first Bishop of Vence, is significant only as a rough approximation. The first church of Vence, to make room for which a temple to Cybele was pulled down, was probably a sort of basilica constructed, perhaps, out of the very blocks that had formed the house of the goddess of fertility.

We do not encounter a clear historical Christian personality in Vence until we meet St. Eusebius, the bishop who went in 376 as an equal with His Grandeur, the Bishop of Arles, and His Grandeur, the Bishop of Nice, to the council at Aquileia, called to fight the growing heresy of Arianism. It was a long, expensive journey for the bishop of a humble little diocese to take, but it is gratifying to civic pride to learn that the bishops arrived at the council with "great *éclat*."

Those were the times when Provence was, so to speak, alive with saints; at least many saints were then alive, but it may have been easier to be a saint in those times than in the wicked nowadays. Miracles were common occurrences, and to live in one of the plentiful caves, to subsist on roots and go about in rags, to abstain from the indulgence of bathing and to have an eye for the mote in one's neighbor's eye— these often went with saintliness, and a prophet, like Salvianus, who howled calamity over the rot in the empire and the apocalypse of the barbarians, could not go far wrong. In those days there were flagellants and cenobites and troglodytes in the land, and men who put away their wives did a godly thing. Pan, long patron of this land of shepherds, was confounded with the Devil, and the Devil, as Salvianus thundered, as Augustine warned in Hippo, as St. Bernard was still telling the world some seven hundred years later, lurked in everything that pleased the senses—in bird song and forest and dew-hung bluebells, in works of art, in cleanliness, in fine raiment and fair women, and even in the ear-flattering charms of church hymns.

At the barbarians' approach many godly and prudent men withdrew into cells and caves, and among those who took up abode in the caves of the Estérel Mountains were two men who, however adorned with legend, are in some measure historical. One was St. Eucherius, who had been a wealthy Gallo-Roman and had put away his wife in order to make them both saints; another was Honoratus, to whom Eucherius told of two uninhabited islands, myrtle-scented and dreaming, off the shore of modern Cannes.

Thither went Honoratus, drove forth the snakes (an

accomplishment he later taught to St. Patrick), and founded there the monastery of the Lérins Islands, which was to be to France what Monte Cassino was to Italy or Fulda to Germany, a beacon light of learning and religious sincerity through the Dark Ages, and a cradle of saints and bishops. Vence, close to its sweet radiance, was to find many of her bishops there, and to look toward the Lérins for guidance in all the calamities that were to come.

For calamity was now at hand. Over the Alps in 411, roaring and slaying, staving the wine vats, looting the towns, counting the women as spoil, came the Visigoths, fresh from the sack of Rome. Though they were thrown back from Marseille defeated, they came again in 420, 430, 434. There was still antique virtue in the Roman power in Gaul. The towns held firm. But in 443 the Burgundians came sweeping down the Rhône Valley, turned east, and laid all this country under their firm but intelligent and Christian rule. Probably Vence opened her gates, paid tribute, made submission.

As the twilight of the Dark Ages deepened into gloom, Vence received a new bishop, St. Veranus, a monk of Lérins and the son of St. Eucherius. Not only his father but his mother, brother, and sisters were all saints, and he had imbibed his faith at the fountain of the Lérins just when the island monastery was at its purest. His gentle figure shed on Vence, ob-

41

scure and poor, the light of merit. Pope Leo the Great himself had no more beloved spiritual son than Veranus, whom he called upon to settle disputes between bishops throughout Gaul. There is extant still a letter from Veranus to Pope Leo, which gives to this Bishop of Vence, hero of innumerable legends, a historical authenticity undeniable. In this epistle Veranus joins the Holy Father in denouncing Eutyches, the sponsor of one more of these passionately hair-splitting differences then proclaimed heresy.

But the shepherd of souls in little Vence was no bloodless theologian. And now a ruder peril than the detestable Eutycheanism threatened his flock. Euric the Goth was marching on Provence. Some say that he had with him Genseric the Vandal when in 476 he drew up his camp near the mouth of the Loup. And Euric was not a tolerant, pagan warrior; he was an Arian Christian, and Veranus and Vence were Athanasians. If Euric had worshiped Thor and Odin, he might have let Vence off for a modest barbaric consideration—say, all the wine, women, and gold in the town. As it was, he was an early Unitarian, and he had vowed destruction to all Trinitarians. Euric was a well-educated man; he spoke better Latin than many Gallo-Romans and wrote essays in that tongue. He knew history and the politics of the empire; he could put his finger on every man's weak spot, and up to the present no one had bested him. So this dangerously intelligent conqueror cast up his eyes toward the cliffs and the columns of Roman Vence, and fingered thoughtfully his sword hilt.

What happened next is legend-like, yet sober historians allow it, and if it seems almost a miracle, then we must set it down as one of those events that sometimes happen when nothing but a miracle would suffice.

For there arose a stir in the camp of the barbarians, and if Euric expected to see cringing messengers from the town in the hills, he was astonished to behold a man in middle life, clad in priestly garments, threading his way through the parted ranks, the bearded warriors, the heaped-up spoils, coffers and chests, silks, rugs, sacks of meal, vats of wine, fine horses, and women with bound hands. It was Veranus, come to beg for mercy. No one knows exactly what words passed between those men, Gallic bishop and Germanic war lord, exchanging speech in resounding Latin while eyes searched eyes for hidden thoughts.

But the miracle occurred; the bishop strode away, humbly rejoicing, and the great captain roared commands. The army moved, caked in the mud and the blood of the wars; the horses moved, wrung and weary under the spoils; the women moved, toward the fate of captive women. And in an hour they had vanished, the tramping of feet no louder than thunder in the Estérels.

Veranus died amongst his flock, on May 10, 492, one of the last of the old Gallo-Romans. Somewhere in the walls or the crypt of his church his dust may still be lying. What they call his tomb is indeed a Roman sarcophagus, but the skull called his, in a golden shrine of modern pious manufacture, may have sat once on anyone's shoulders. It matters little what outward thing is worshiped in his name, so that he be remembered. There is, indeed, a whole mythology of the beloved figure called "Sant Vrain." Many Provençal cities claim that he was once their bishop, but only Vence has historical justification for this claim. The most entertaining of the Sant Vrain legends is that he brought a wicked dragon to confession and tears of repentance.

Burgundian and Visigothic power came to an end toward 510, when Amalaric ceded Provence to Theodoric, king of the Italian Ostrogoths, in return for help against the Franks. Of whatever the Ostrogoths may have wrought in Vence there is no record, but they must have shed on the land a few last gleams from the flickering lamp of the classic world. Long resident in Greece and Italy, the Ostrogoths were the most civilized of the barbarians, and when the Visigoths and Franks sought to recapture Provence, it stood firm for its wise masters the Ostrogoths. Not till 537 did Clovis the Frank purchase Provence from Witigis the Ostrogoth for twenty thousand *ecus* of pure gold. Nominally Vence then became Frankish. But though one hears the names of Frankish kings who held it in fief—Clotair and Childibert, Gontram and Sigibert—their capitals were far away, and their sway was feeble.

It was in these days that Bishop Firmin led his flock. Again a Bishop of Vence has been called into a position of world note, for he was one of the fourteen delegates to the Second Council of Orange (529), one of the most important gatherings of the sixth century. Though primarily the delegates were come together to dedicate a church, they took up here one of the fundamental issues in human faith—the question of predestination to evil versus divine mercy. Thus little Vence wielded an influence of lasting importance upon religious thought.

Ever since the second century the predestinarian controversy had been growing in the Church, and it was no hair-splitting matter like most of the antique heresies. There were those in that stern era who found, in the Augustinian declarations of corruption and human inability, support for the dark idea that some men are predestined to evil by God himself. While reaffirming the Augustinian doctrines, this earnest conclave of Bishop Firmin and his colleagues, under the presidency of the vigorous Caesarius, made vehement denial of the notion that God could damn to evil any mortal soul. Across the centuries their protestation breathes still fresh and warm: "That some are by the divine power predestinated to evil, we not only do not believe, but, also, if there are any who are willing to believe such a wicked thing, we say to them *anathema*, with every possible abhorrence."

But once again questions of ethic vanish before the sword. Over the Alps in 573 came the terrible Lombards, with the will to wipe out everything that bore the stamp of Rome. Roman bridges, columns, aqueducts, villas, theaters, inscriptions—all must go. Much that was Roman had survived every storm; now all who spoke the Latin tongue should be put to the sword. The tombs of the saints were thrown open and desecrated. The nuns of Arluc (who had neglected the precaution of cutting off their noses, like some near Marseille) were parceled out for revelry. Cimiez, which may have had sixty thousand inhabitants, was destroyed. The monastery called the Doriade, placed where Veranus had turned back the Goth, ran red with monkish blood. Vence too was given to the flames, and her people fled to their *bastide*, the fortress on the *baou*. Defeated on the Rhône, the Lombards went back to Italy, to return again in 580 and remain.

This is the deep midnight of the Dark Ages.

Good Bishop Deutheric persuaded the terrified Vençois to come down from the *bastide* and rebuild their town. It must have been built out of the fire-blackened stones of the Roman city; it must have been a poorer town, a meaner town, huddled together, a town without art, without sunlight.

With War and Fire in the land, Famine could not be far behind, and when it came it lasted eight years. Last of the Apocalyptic horsemen, late, but riding hard, came Pestilence, with fever rolling like opal fire in his eyes, and his gaunt horse covered with sores. Under his hoofs Roman and Frank bowed down, and even the Lombard was sobered, made common cause with the people he had harried, took their religion, and mingled his blood with theirs. Many a doughty Templar, many a blue-eyed woman, descended from the Lombard strain.

Provence had been invaded from every direction except the south. Now across the seas came the first Arab ships from Africa. The Crescent was waxing to its full. The children of the desert in the seventh century had swept along the coast of North Africa, carrying the Byzantine and Vandal kingdoms down as a wave carries away weak piers. It is said that when the mere name of the Arabs was spoken, Rodriguez, last of the old kings of Spain, trembled on his throne. Now virtually all Spain is lost to Christendom, and the western horn of the Crescent has pierced the side of France. The Saracenic hosts washed over Gascony. The towns of Languedoc suffered a whirlwind destruction. In quiet cities of today,

47

Montpellier, Béziers, and Albi, tens of thousands of souls were shorn from the shrieking bodies they inhabited. The cities of the Rhône Valley, except a few strong ones, succumbed to the right flank of this invasion; in our eastern Provence the first depredations of the Saracens were largely, I think, by sea raids.

In 720 Charles Martel, "Charles the Hammer," struck the Arabs in Provence. But it was like striking the surface of the sea. They were back in 731, and the following year a monster invasion, comparable to no force that ever invaded France save the Huns and the Germans, marched on Paris. At Poitiers in 732 Charles Martel won a mighty victory; the Saracens retired to Languedoc.

But in that same year Christianity suffered irreparable loss. Across the sea the long feluccas came, landing a host on the island of St. Honorat. Porcarius, abbot of the Lérins monastery, marched out to meet the paynim ranks at the head of five hundred monks— singing men, unarmed, going toward martyrs' death. All but two who hid were slain; the monastery fell in ashes; the light of learning was put out.

Charles Martel four times struck the Arabs in Provence, the last time in 739; four times they returned. The demoralization of terror settled on the land; the story becomes confused; dates are at variance or unreliable. I could not record all the Saracenic raids upon this countryside; knight and peasant, priest and boy, were slain; church and maid were ravished; the bricks of cities sent up bitter smoke.

Picture the moonless night, the grounding of the stealthy ships, the passage of dark men through the dark night—Arab commanders, squat Berber rascals, dregs of the crumbled kingdoms of North Africa. Imagine the sentry's cry, the plunderers' yells, the fighting in the streets. Of history there is pitifully little to relate; it is easy to amplify the horrid probabilities.

By the year 813 Vence had been raided; its inhabitants no doubt fled away to their *bastide* in the mountains. By 891 the country around Toulon was as Saracen as Arabia; to this day the mountains there are called the Montagnes des Maures. Then the paynims cross the Estérels, not as raiders now but as conquerors who meant to stay. The infidel tide washed to the very Alps; monasteries considered remote from all danger, whither sacred relics had been sent for safety, were assaulted. Vence must have shared in this final eclipse by the moon of Araby; the little town is swallowed by black night a century long. For more than a hundred years there will be no recorded mention of Vence; no more bishops, no priests, no churches, no knights, no Christian houses or farms or freemen.

The list of the bishops of Vence at the end of this chapter tells the tale. The gap in the chronology which falls in the year 644 may indicate the destruction by the Lombards, or, as Tisserand suggests, a usurpation of churchly power by the congregation, or merely lost records. But the gap that follows the name of Élie, who came to the see of Vence in 879, means only one thing—the cruel paynim conquest. Élie, of course, is but the French rendering of the name Elijah. Was the Elijah of Vence a white-haired old prophet of destruction too? And was he too snatched up to heaven in the fiery chariot of holocaust? Or was he slain at his altar, or did he fall at the galley oars?

Dark was the fate of Provence in the first drunken triumphs of the Arabs, when the nuns of Arluc graced a harem. But while the Christians hid in caves and rock forts, the Arabs began to settle the land after their own liking. Despite the patriotic French historians, who ascribe nothing but murder and rapine to the Arabs, these swarthy folk were a gifted race, and they are an integral part of the long pageantry of the peoples who have loved and wooed Provence and made her bear them fruit.

First the Arabs built them forts or *rebbaths*, from which they sent out armed bands to bring in gold and slaves. Then towns arose, and farms. Provence began to blossom as never before in her long history. As a husbandman the Arab had a distinguished tradition. Not only did he introduce the *abaran* olive to take its

50

place beside the Greek type, but he brought to these terraces sugar cane and rice, which no one else has ever succeeded in growing here. To him are owed saffron, safflower, the cork oak, the carob (Arabic: *karouba*), buckwheat (French: *sarrasin*), date palms, possibly silk worms and the mulberry. The windmill made its first appearance and was used to irrigate thousand of miles of terraces. It is said that Provence owes the damask or Damascus rose and the porous water jar to the Arab. Today around Vence roses are a major crop; the great jars, big enough to drown one of Ali Baba's thieves in, stand under the olives all about my house.

During the Arabic occupation the pointed arch made its appearance in Provence, long antedating the Gothic, which is a style that has never gained any ground upon these shores. Old houses of Tourrettes and Vence confess by many a pointed arch the paynim influence. The *mauresques* (English: Morris) dances are certainly of Arabic origin, and the long drum to which Provençals dance the *mauresques* is Moorish too. Provence in those distant days shared in the whole of the Damascene renaissance, when astronomy, geography, algebra, medicine, botany, poetry, music, and architecture flourished where the Crescent waxed.

So for some one hundred and fifty years this part of

51

Provence was lost to France.[1] The kings of Arles and the dukes of Burgundy held but empty titles to it. The country was almost delivered by Hugues, or Hugo, Marquis of Provence, but he gave up Provence to keep Italy. Not until 975 did forces gather for the final delivery of Provence. Led by Brother Majolus (St. Mayeul), a monk of Cluny who had once been a Saracen slave, the knights of southern France took heart. Among them were Isarn, Bishop of Grenoble (bishops were proud to hack off paynim heads in those days), and Bava of Sisteron, whose wife had been ravished by an Arab, and Gibelin Grimaldi, a nephew of Pépin and ancestor of the present Prince of Monaco. Their leader was Rouvaud, or Rotbold, brother to Count William I of Provence, who generally gets the credit and spelled his name, if he could write (which is doubtful), Guillhaulme. Aided by Otho the Great of Germany, the Franks took the *rebbaths* of the Moors, one by one. For ten long years the struggle passed from stronghold to stronghold, with desperate fighting until the last paynim was stricken to his knees.

And, since the Saracens are now to pass from the scene, a last word may be said about Saracenic blood

[1] The assertion that Charlemagne passed this way, either to fight the paynim or to take his road to Rome, is proved the invention of a monk of St. Pons, at Nice. This fabrication was embroidered by the historian Toselli, was believed by Tisserand, and has been included by Giraud in his book on Vence.

among the Vençois. In Cannes they tell you that the Vençois are contaminated with this heathen strain, that the people of Vence are *"méchants,"* tricky, tough, a reputation that dates back to the Middle Ages, when they were feared at fairs for their heavy drinking, their readiness with their fists, knives, and scythes. Although it is now biologically impossible that any Saracenic blood could persist in traces sufficient to give racial characteristics to the population, probably some of the medieval Vençois had Saracen blood. Whether it would be a disgrace to be descended from the race that bore Haroun the Just and Averrhoës, the great healer, might be debatable. But it is inconceivable, in the century when the Arabs were masters and the Christians slaves, that Frankish women hereabout were not compelled to bear swarthy sons and daughters. And the legend of the Arab chief Haroun of St. Agnès who turned Christian for love of a shepherd's daughter has the historical value of all legends, a value superior to a mere fact, for the one tale tells a thousand. The moral of them all is that Provence has conquered all its conquerors. As late as the middle of the thirteenth century there were paynims in Vence, for the Seigneur Roumiou makes mention in his will (1250) of his Saracen men and women slaves.

So the light of the Damascene lamp goes out. And

very feebly the trodden rushlight of Provençal Christianity flickers again, catches with stronger flame, and paints the walls of Vence with new and gorgeous colors.

CHRONOLOGY FOR CHAPTER THREE

END OF THE ROMAN EMPIRE IN THE WEST

363 Jovianus
364 Valentinianus
375 Gratianus and Valentinianus II
388 Theodosius the Great, already emperor of the East, re-unites the empire
395 Honorius, emperor of the West
424 Valentinian III
455 Valentinian III dies and is followed by "phantom emperors," the last of whom,
476 Romulus Augustulus, is deposed by the barbarian Odoacer
The Western empire is at an end

FRANKISH KINGS

The Merovingian Line

481 Clovis
511 Clotaire
628 Dagobert
638 *et seq*. The "Do-Nothing Kings"

The Carlovingian Line

752 Pépin the Short
768 Charlemagne
814 Louis the Debonaire
843 Charles the Bald
877 Louis the Stammerer
879 Carloman

888 Eudes or Odo
898 Charles III, the Fool
922 Robert I
923 Raoul
936 Louis IV d'Outremer
954 Lothair I
986 Louis V

RULERS OF PROVENCE

510 Amalaric the Visigoth cedes Provence to Theodoric the Ostrogoth
537 Witigis the Ostrogoth cedes Provence to the Frankish Kings
700 Arab conquest begins
843 Lothair I, Emperor of the Franks, receives Provence at the Partition of Verdun and sets up for his son Charles the Kingdom of Provence
863 Louis II, Emperor in Italy (brother of Charles, the son of Lothair)

"Kings of Arles" (Provence)

875 Duke Boso (brother-in-law of Charles the Bald) reconstitutes the Kingdom of Provence
890 Louis the Blind (died in 928 without legitimate heir)
929 Hugues or Hugo, "Marquis of Provence and King of Italy"

Sovereign Counts of Provence

923 Boso or Boson I
945 Boso II
961 Guillaume I

BISHOPS OF VENCE

250? Audinus?
     No records until:
374 Eusebius
410 Juvenius
430 Arcadius

55

451 Veranus
492 Prosper
535 Firmin
541 Deutherius
588 Fronymus
644 Aurelien
        No records until:
835 Lieutaud
877 Valdine
878 Vilfride
879 Elie
        No further records for a hundred and twenty years.

Chapter Four

THE MIDDLE AGES

FROM THE EXPULSION OF THE SARACENS TO THE EXPULSION OF THE TEMPLARS

AT SOME DATE CLOSE TO THE YEAR 1000 THE TOWN of Vence must have been raised again. There is nothing Gallo-Roman left. Pure medievalism, with all its panoply and poetry, its misery and bigotry, sweeps upon the scene. The free, logical toga gives place to the fantastic armor of the knight. Europe has pulled down its visor; from the suspicious slits its eyes look out upon the world, contemptuous of book learning, superstitiously respectful toward monks and priests, avid of fair women. The people of Vence, the common people, are now a Provençal people, a thorough mixture of Frank and Burgundian, Lombard, Visigoth, and Ostrogoth. And Provençal culture is becoming the keystone in the cultural arch of the western Mediterranean stretching from Spain to Italy. Vence, contrary to common remark, has nothing Italian about it; Italian was never spoken here, nor was the dialect even modified by that tongue. On the contrary, Provençal is in many respects the aristocrat of all living Romance languages, closer to classic Latin than Italian, French, or Spanish. Early Provençal customs, costumes, architecture, and literature were unaffected by Italy; rather, that adjacent land took color from Provence. Petrarch, in Avignon, learned from the troubadours.

When Count William of Provence by right of arms became the lord of the country from which the Saracens had been driven, he divided up with his nobles the spoils of the land, or rather he allowed them to enjoy tracts and fiefs in consideration of their becoming his vassals; and so, in orthodox style, Provence entered into that social and economic scheme called feudalism. Already on the roster of the liberators of Provence appear the family names that figure through the history of Vence and its neighborhood—names that will sound in all the clash of arms, that will be linked with pomp in the well-preserved records of marriages. Such are Blacas of Carros, which Good King René was to call a synonym for valor, and one Raymond de Villa Nova, of whose family much more anon.

The town of Vence itself is mentioned as part of the dowry which the noble damozel Odille, daughter of Count William, brought to her husband, Laugier Ruffi. And it is about this time that the name of Bishop Arnoul appears in the chronicles of Vence—a legendary bishop, perhaps, by strict historical criteria, but under the Saracens history had been bare even of legends.

In and about the new settlement at Vence there were at this time only two great powers, the bishops and the barons or seigneurs. As yet neither peasant nor townsman has any rights worth mentioning, though these humbler folk were not molested in their work or play providing that they paid what was asked of them, believed what was preached to them, and died when they were ordered to.

The seigneurs undertook on their side to protect the town and peasantry by force of arms, though only as commanders. The town and the peasants did the fighting and often paid the expenses. No one might leave the land or the profession in which he was born without permission of the liege, and among his dues the noble claimed not only taxes but workmen for all sorts of labor, and a large caste of women serfs and children in domestic service.

The terms of feudal contract stipulated that the

lord might demand contributions yearly of wine, oil, wood, meat, fruit, cereals, shoulders of venison, hams of boar. Yet townsmen and peasants were forbidden to cut wood, hunt,[1] or even pick berries or firewood on all the best land or to fish in the streams thereto appertaining. The peasant family met such conditions by living close to starvation; the townsman groaned, but opened his coffers. Vence would have been defenseless against its seigneurs had it not been, despite its small size, a cathedral city, with bishops to offset the puissance of the seigneurs.

For bishops were not less powerful than nobles. The prelates also claimed trout streams, chestnut groves, fruit orchards, rents, and even oil mills and corn mills, all left them by the wills of repentant sinners. So it came about that the bishops of Vence were co-seigneurs with the secular nobles in the fiefs of Vence, just as the abbots of the Lérins were rated as among the foremost landowners of Provence. And not unnaturally the bishops often found their material interests in conflict with the rights of the seigneurs. If the noble could have recourse to the battle-ax and could claim the protection of his liege, the Count of Provence, so the bishop could appeal to Rome, and he had his sacerdotal buttresses of priests, curates, can-

[1] Game foods of the Middle Ages in Vence are shown by the records to have been quail, grouse, partridge, turtledove, woodcock, pigeon, thrush, wild boar, deer, and bear. Foxes and lynxes furnished sport for the noble huntsman. Falconry was a favorite pastime.

ons, and even an armed bodyguard, to match the baron's villains, varlets, and men-at-arms.

It was in the effort of bishop and baron to play off the town of Vence one against the other, to win the burgesses' favor by granting them privileges, that the commune of Vence was little by little to gain its independence. Sometimes it inclined toward its baron, more often to its bishop, who generally had the interests of the people more sincerely at heart. And slipping thus between its two lords it emerged greater than they.

But that time is almost eight hundred years off. And we are now just breathing freely after the year 1000 has passed without the end of the world so confidently predicted. Pons, a holy man sent to gentle the eleventh-century Vençois, finds them "rudes et totius boni ignaros ac religiones." Pons it was who, hatchet in hand, cut down the jungle of shrubs and brambles on the deserted site of the Doriade monastery, where Veranus had turned back the Goth. For the new monastery the Count of Vence and Odille, his wife, gave lands and money.

It was in the middle of the twelfth century that Vence had once again a saint for a bishop, the last of its holy men and, with St. Veranus, one of its two patron saints. Bishop Lambert, born in 1084 at Bauduen in Provence, of the noble family of Pelloquin, had, so tradition says, been sent at the age of twelve to the abbey of the Lérins,[2] whence he was called to Vence. Unlike Veranus, he did not figure in councils; indeed he seldom left his oratory to congregate with other mitered heads. He washed the leper and he plowed with his own hand, and never ceased from mortifying his flesh.

On Good Friday, while his canons were dining and he was eating nothing, his water suddenly turned to wine. He called a servant to take it away, thinking that a mistake had been made, but thrice the cup glowed ruby. The practical Vençois kept this wine for many a year, and it was rumored to be of a most excellent *goût*, but the supply diminished without any member of the chapter caring to say just how; it is now inquired for in vain.

Other miracles of Lambert were more significant. A blind woman of Nice who touched his robes regained her sight. When he died in 1154, so great was the crowd of his mourners that they became a mob and had to be managed by soldiers. He was placed in a tomb from which presently water flowed; in this the pious bathed, and the infirm so found themselves healed of their diseases. It is a poor Mediterranean church that cannot boast similar miracles, and altogether St. Lambert, though he lived six hundred

[2] So far as I have discovered, there is no record of his residence at the Lérins. Lack of record would not disprove it, but it increases one's feeling that the real Lambert is obscured behind a legend that is a sort of composite portrait of old bishops.

years closer to our times, is a much more shadowy and less historical personality than Veranus. The Dark Ages have done their beclouding work quite thoroughly, and, in place of the stern courage and intellectuality of fifth-century Christianity, we have now the mysticism and credulity of the twelfth.

That mysticism and credulity, indeed, were firing Europe with the spirit of the Crusades, and in those days all classes, noble and varlet, fugitive from justice, boys in search of excitement, priests, hermits, women both sacred and profane, and even children, were hurrying to buy themselves a place in divine salvation. What part the people of Vence played in the drama on Syrian sands I cannot say,[3] but it was a movement especially appealing to the Provençal spirit, and Provençals crowded the ranks of the two great militant orders, the Knights Hospitalers of St. John and the Knights of the Temple.

But while the pageant defiled toward Jerusalem, the danger of the paynim was close at hand. Saracenic raiders from Africa had never ceased to ravage the coasts of Provence (indeed, they came as late as 1830!), and the towns of Cannes, Antibes, and La Napoule were repeatedly burned and plundered. The chief object of the raids may well have been women, as tradition states, who were sold all through the

[3] They certainly took part in the last Crusade, but this was directed against Tunis. In the first Crusade it was a Provençal, some say a native of St. Paul, who planted the Christian standard on the walls of Acre.

Near East and North Africa, though gold and strong young men came not amiss, and Allah was doubtless pleased if a bishop could be captured or a church stripped and desecrated.

To meet this danger, the Count of Provence established the Templars all along the coast. And, by purchase from their well-filled coffers and by legacy, they acquired the rights in farms and vineyards, mills, forests, fishing streams, until their wealth and power were as notorious as their courage. The whole of eastern Provence was embraced in the Priory of St. Giles, and it numbered fifty-four commanderies. Their strong-towers were so numerous around Vence that they were seldom out of sight of each other, and thus, at the first glimpse of a far felucca, signal fires could be lighted to summon aid from the more distant mountain fortresses.

Many of the Templars' houses about Vence were fortified châteaux, and must have been sumptuously furnished in all the comfortless splendor of the Middle Ages. They were set in the midst of green meads blowing with narcissus and anemone, and always looked either on the sea or on the Alps, and frequently on both. One of the mightiest was at Pennafort, on the banks of the Loup; this property was a gift to the puissant order from the abbots of the Lérins, for at that time (1137) the island monastery was in the heyday of its worldly prosperity, holding all the coast from the Estérels to the mouth of the Loup in fee—much to the annoyance of the bishops of Grasse. The master-house of the Templars hereabout was the commandery of St. Martin, whose imposing ruins today rise bleakly halfway up the slopes of the Baou des Pénitents Blancs just above Vence. Appended to it was the grange of St. Raphaël, which still stands on the mountain of that name—a lonely tower of broken stone grown over now with prying ivy and legend. And a long tramp out of Vence will take you to the great château of the Templars between St. Jeannet and La Gaude, set like a giant's chess castle on its round green hill. Built by the Knights in 1125, it has defied war and weather, so that the doughty walls still frown upon the innocent surrounding country-side, though valerian and bluebell, campion and dusty miller, have come to perch impertinently in the crannies.

This stronghold looked down upon the tragedy of a hapless people who pass here like shadows across the history of Vence. The bare facts record that in 1215 the hamlet of Allaganza (La Gaude) was burned by order of Count Raymond Bérenger, for harboring the Albigensian heretics. Given but twenty-four hours to quit Provence, these hunted people paused in the shadow of the *baous* while on their flight toward Italy, or rather to Sospel, where many of them were burned. The old Catholic writers, who treat all heresies as if they were one, confuse the Albigensians with the Vaudois, but the Vaudois were a peasant sect, with stern, reasonable tenets that may have given Calvin his ideas and resembled the faith of John Huss, while the Albigensians were the very flower of the nobility and chivalry of Languedoc— the gentlest and most refined folk in all of Europe. What they really believed we may never know, for we have only their oppressors' word for it. The Church says they were contaminated with gnosticism and catharism. In case this does not convince you that they deserved to be burned, I'm sure I have only to add that they were riddled with Manichean doctrines.

Through the eleventh, twelfth, and thirteenth centuries the life of this land went on like an old tale. Visored knights, clanking in armor, spurred across the flowery fields; lord warred with lord from hilltop castles. On moonless nights a felucca from Barbary might drop anchor in the bay, surprise a rock village, carry off its women. All the Provençal life and background found in *Aucassin and Nicolette* was the daily existence and environment of the folk of Vence. It was the age of chivalry, par excellence, when what we are pleased to call "romance" was simple reality.

Not that the code of chivalry had much to do with womankind. Woman, always the property of her father or her husband, had little disposition, if she obeyed the dictates of society, over her mind or body. The one field permitted to her play instinct was found in the "Courts of Love," a very Provençal institution, a sort of parlor game that nobody took seriously, which spread into France and Italy among women of the leisured class. Here, in pretense, ladies of melodious names had the world as they would have liked it, chivalrous in the modern sense of the word. The troubadour[4] improvising a romantic poem was the lady's substitute for light novels. Her little sentimental court was composed of poets, squires who had not won their spurs, maids, and pages.

The lady's husband represented a more or less stern reality with which she became conjugally acquainted, with or without her leave, at earliest nubility, or often before. He might be a clanking, gristle-gnawing fellow who held her brains in contempt, chastised her like a child, and locked her up; he might be illiterate and superstitious; but he had, no doubt, his tendernesses; he was prepared to die for her honor and he provided her with the luxuries of the day. A wife with a pretty face, money, and powerful kinsmen held sway in her feminine way, and if she was fertile she was respected and indispensable. A noblewoman left a widow, who knew how to manage

[4] Vence had no native troubadour so far as I know. But Grasse boasts Bellaud de la Bellaudière (1532–88), whose *Obras e rimos* was the first book printed in Provence (1585). Troubadouring was a pastime with him; his profession was highway robbery, and he died upon the gallows, another Villon.

men and could control her sons, might easily prove the most powerful person in the community, and the history of Vence offers several examples of such women.

Some such there were in the great reigning family of Vence which now sweeps upon its little stage. The way is cleared for the Villeneuves by one of those local uprisings that are but bubbles in the seething caldron of Europe. The old Seigneur of Vence, Guillaume d'Esparon, and the Seigneur Aymonet of Malvans joined in a movement of rebellion against the Count of Provence, Raymond Bérenger. Grasse and Draguignan went into it too, plotting for the independence of eastern Provence from the rest, with Nice as a possible capital. Into the scheme came the intriguing free merchant-city of Genoa, and the Count of Provence might have lost much but for the loyal support of Roumiou de Villa Nova (in French, Romée de Villeneuve), who was grand seneschal of Provence. At his dread approach toward the rebellious towns, their resistance wilted.

In return for his services the trouble-making seigneurs were in 1230 dispossessed, and he was enfeoffed, by his liege the Count, with a block of fiefs that included Vence, Malvans, Cagnes, St. Jeannet, La Gaude, Loubet, Antibes, Grasse, Le Puget du Var, St. Laurent du Var, Coursegoules, Cipières, and Thorenc. Partition among sons and daughters presently diminished this handsome holding, so that the map of that great fief of which Vence was at first the capital was constantly changing. Notably Grasse, Antibes, Cagnes, and Loubet were soon detached and had their own seigneurs who were at least as powerful as the Villeneuve-Vence, but in general the seigneurs of Vence always held the land between the Loup and the Estéron except at the mouths and headwaters of those rivers.

Roumiou de Villa Nova (1190?–1251) was the first of the seigneurs Villeneuve who ruled with a strong hand in Vence from 1230 until the French Revolution. There were twenty-six of them including the last, who came after the Revolution and during the Bourbon restoration, and it must have been a gifted line, intelligent, forceful, with strong administrative talents. Though their political acts and the spots where they dwelt and the châteaux they built are well known, their personalities are unfortunately obscure. Yet remote as it is, Roumiou's life stands out in vivid colors, partly the colors of legend, partly those of history, and alone among the seigneurs of Vence he attained national and immortal fame—national because as grand seneschal to the great Raymond Bérenger he appears in Larousse, and immortal because Dante put him in *Paradiso*.

Roumiou's birthplace is not certainly known, but it was probably at Trans or Arcs-en-Provence, just

69

south of Draguignan, and it seems certain that he was a *cadet* of the house of Villeneuve de Trans et d'Arcs, son of Giraud the seigneur of those places and bailiff of Antibes. This particular clan of the Villeneuves was obscure at the time, rustic and poor. But the Villeneuve family would easily rank as one of the first six families of Provence; it has venerable connections in Aragon, where it originated, and was once distinguished in England. Among the Provençal Villeneuves are the Admiral Villeneuve, who was honorably defeated by Nelson at Trafalgar, and Hélion, the grand master of Malta, who defeated Suleiman the Magnificent. Hélion's sister was St. Roseleyne. And we may note Louis, *"Riche d'honneur,"* who was chamberlain to Francis I, ambassador to Rome, and friend of Bayard. "Master Arnaud," born at Villeneuve-Loubet, was the alchemist and doctor who discovered sulphuric, muriatic, and nitric acids and on account of his endeavors to scrutinize the Inscrutable was excommunicated, until the pope fell sick, when it became advisable to lift the excommunication and send in a hurry for Master Arnaud, who died upon the way. The escutcheon of this notable tribe shows a red field fretted with six golden lances, crossed, with small shields between, and in the center a golden *fleur-de-lis* upon a field of azure.

Roumiou had little chance, as a young brother, of inheriting his father's stony little fief. But he was destined to glory, though at this point tradition and history part company and seldom, in the tale of Roumiou, meet again even at his death. According to the legends on which Dante drew, Roumiou was a poor pilgrim who had journeyed to the Holy Land and on his return was wandering in the streets of Grasse when Count Raymond Bérenger first met him and fell under the spell of his manner "and the graceful sentiments that accompanied his talk." A great talker was Roumiou, and an eager listener was his Count, and many a long hour the pilgrim whiled away, telling of his travels—of nobles fighting in the dark streets of Florence, of the tower of Pisa (before it leaned), and the sea birds round the white cliffs of England; of flowers that bloom in the alpine snows, "of the hiving of bees, and of the curious ways of women."

By degrees he rose to be grand seneschal and bailiff of Provence, constable and minister of state and chancellor of the exchequer. But if Roumiou was goodly in the sight of the Count, he was hateful to the nobles; he clipped their wings wherever he went, and, to counterbalance their power, so dangerous to his master, he gave to merchants, towns and ports, important rights. Vence may have received her first real civic liberties at his hands.

Legend goes further; it tells us how the nobles poisoned the ear of the Count; they inquired, with un-

71

pleasant implication, for a statement from the chancellor of his expenditures of the state's moneys; they dared the Count to ask what was kept in that box of Roumiou's that was never opened.

The Count at last consented; with a wounded look Roumiou opened the box. It contained nothing but the pilgrim's habit and staff which had been his when first he met his beloved master. Weeping, the Count begged forgiveness. "I forgive you willingly," said Roumiou, "but my heart is broken." And sadly he donned the pilgrim's habit once more, left the court, and wandered the land, begging his way.

This story never seemed to me more credible or more dramatic than the little bit of truth that we know about Roumiou. He was, historically, a young nobleman of the more rustic group of eastern Provence, who, ambitious and aware of his capabilities, placed his services at the disposal of his Count. He helped his lord to organize his finances, kept the estates intact, and when need came took up the sword. When the galleys of Provence, ferrying a bevy of cardinals to Rome, were scattered by the fleet of the Emperor Frederick II, the pope-hater, only Roumiou kept his squadron in order, and even brought back a captured ship. When the Count desired to codify the laws of Provence, it was Roumiou who, with the Bishop of Fréjus and two ministers of state, drew up the Statutes of Fréjus. You may see in the treasure of the church at St. Paul the alleged original of that document by which Provence was long to live.

The master-stroke in medieval diplomacy was frequently a strong dynastic marriage. Roumiou made four such master-strokes, for though the Count of Provence considered himself accursed with nothing but daughters, Roumiou contrived to wed Marguerite to St. Louis, King of France, Elenore to Henry III of England, Blanche to his brother Richard, and Béatrix, the youngest, to Charles of Anjou, brother to the King of France. At least he arranged the betrothals (Béatrix was playing with dolls at the time). He made his will in 1250 and, dying the next year, was buried in the Church of the Dominicans at Nice. The chroniclers of Vence claim that he breathed his last in the town's old château. It may be so, but the château is much altered since those days, and what, anyway, does it matter, since Dante has built him a mansion in Paradise?

> Within the pearl, that now encloseth us,
> Shines Romeo's light, whose goodly deed and fair
> Met ill acceptance. But the Provençals,
> That were his foes, have little cause for mirth.
> Ill shapes that man his course who makes his wrong
> Of others' worth. Four daughters were there born
> To Raymond Bérenger: and every one
> Became a queen: and this for him did Romeo,
> Though of mean state and from a foreign land.
> Yet envious tongues incited him to ask
> A reckoning of that just one, who returned

73

Twelve fold to him for ten. Aged and poor
He parted thence: and if the world did know
The heart he had, begging his life by morsels,
'T would deem the praise it yields him scantly dealt.[5]

Such was the founder of the great family of Vence's seigneurs, and so it was that Provence passed to the Angevine line, the dukes of Anjou and Provence, who later bore the title of kings of the Two Sicilies (which meant Sicily proper and Naples or the southern third of Italy).

As Seigneur of Vence, Roumiou was succeeded by his son Paul I, who had been one of the hundred knights chosen by Charles of Anjou to attend him in his famous duel with the King of Aragon, and who accompanied St. Louis, King of France, upon the "last Crusade," that tragic expedition against Tunis. Paul, like his brother and sister, failed to fulfil the wishes of his dead father, expressed in the will dated 1250. This instrument provided that Roumiou's daughter Béatrix should enter a convent, that his younger son, Pierre, should become a monk, and that enough of his estates should be sold to pay his debts, with one-fourth of them to be left to the Church. Small wonder if young nobles of high spirit found the fate thus ordained too dreary to accept. Instead, Béatrix married the mighty Hugh de Baux. Pierre, after dutifully becoming a Dominican friar, was to

[5] *The Divine Comedy*, Canto VI.

sally forth into secular life again, in due time to succeed as fourth Seigneur of Vence and beget an heir.

Paul, the second seigneur, in his day continually delayed the disposition of the Villeneuve estates. Had he not done so, he would, presumably, have had no heritage. As it was, the partial sale of the fief reduced it from a large one to a relatively insignificant holding, and as for giving up one-fourth of all he possessed to the Church, Paul flatly declined. As a consequence he was embroiled in a lawsuit and, presently, excommunicated by Bishop Guillaume de Sisteron. But the excommunication does not seem to have been as effective as the prelate surely intended it to be, for Paul remained popular with his subjects and high in the favor of the Count. It was his son Roumiou II, by his young wife, Aicarde de Castellane, who in 1300, by a letter still extant, was to restore to the bishops and the chapter that one-fourth of the Villeneuve inheritance which his grandfather had promised them.

The Angevines, who were all brilliant and more than half of them dangerous, raised Provence, with Anjou and Naples, for a while to power, with castle keeps on every hill, with ambassadors at foreign courts, with expensive navies and expensive queens. It will be for Vence an illustrious period, full of the stir of arms, the bluster of events.

But the reign of Charles of Anjou, first of the Angevine counts, showed Provence the cost of glory.

The Provençal nobles, at the height of their power and drunk with it, swaggered in all the best offices, offending the Italian subjects of Charles. Resentment at his oppressive reign broke out in the Sicilian Vespers (Easter, 1282), where all but one of the great Provençal nobles were massacred. When Charles heard the news, he gnawed his scepter in his rage and grief.

Provence brooded on revenge, though upon the great chessboard of Europe's politics she had little more power than a pawn. And the pope moved her. He preached a "Crusade" to punish the Two Sicilies. The willing and ambitious Charles called on the hill towns for valor. Vence and her neighbors gave the trees for the galleys which Nice built. Every noble family took pride in arming a company. Paul de Villeneuve of Vence raised a contingent—knights in armor, yeomen with their crossbows, boys as pages. With a fine flourish of trumpets the "Crusaders" marched to Nice, to embark for Sicily. When the "Crusade" was over, Paul de Villeneuve lay dead before the walls of Naples; the galleys of Provence were sunk or scattered; the gold was gone; six thousand sons of eastern Provence returned no more.

Meantime the real Crusades were drawing to a dismal close. St. Louis, King of France, had died—not gloriously on the field of battle, but on a bed of fever, slain by the climate of North Africa. Thither the

Seigneur of Vence had loyally followed him, that stubborn and spirited Paul who too was dead now in a foreign field. For Vence, for Provence, the gold was going off a once glittering cause. Even the great order of the Templars could not now say that it had never retreated and never been defeated. It no longer held an inch of territory in the Holy Land. The Knights Hospitalers of Jerusalem, or Johannite Knights, were driven to the island of Rhodes. The majestic folly of the Crusades, unwieldy as a two-handed blade and as slaughterous, was over.

The nobility of Europe, and above all the nobility of Provence, which had poured out its human and material treasure for the Crusades, was practically ruined. Wise and strong old lords, promising, handsome young men, lay dead in Syria. Noble families mortgaged land and castle to the Jews, or sold to towns and merchants their ancient rights. The armor of the feudal system was pierced in a dozen places.

Though the Church had suffered slight loss of prestige through the Crusades, it was not the Church, in little Vence, that gained most by the diminished puissance of the nobles. It was the town and commune. For the churches were many of them in ruin at this time, a consequence of the economic bleeding of Provence. And all along the coast the Turkish pirates swarmed; they were so bold that the pope was obliged to move the bishop from the old seat of Antibes on the coast to Grasse in the mountains. Thereby began one of those medieval and much-enjoyed feuds of the Church. The bishops of Grasse and Vence were from that time forward hereditary enemies, covertly at least, each always ready to encroach upon the spiritual or temporal bailiwick of the other, and jealous in turn of encroachment.

The reign of Charles the Miserly brought better times, for "miserly" was the medieval interpretation of balancing the budget. He was also known as Charles the Lame, and he spent his time in paying off his father's debts. And while Charles practiced thrift, Philip the Fair, of France, who also had debts, thought of a sweeping way of paying them. He decided to kill the fatted calf, his guests the Templars.

For the Templars, being an international organization with castles all the way from Ireland to Cyprus and from Denmark to Armenia, were the great bankers of their age. The Paris Temple was the mightiest money market in Europe; kings and popes deposited their moneys with the Templars, and these were not hoarded but kept in circulation by loans. But now that the Crusades were over and the peril of raiding Saracens past, it was not longer needful to the State to see these rich and arrogant knights in power. And the King's fingers itched.

To reach that magnificent treasure, the order's thick walls must be breached and broken. Philip began to whip up the smoldering embers of scandal and dislike which so secret and so powerful an organization had inevitably bred. It was whispered against the Templars that they bowed down before Baphomet, and worshiped toads; there were unpleasant suggestions in Provence about the disappearance of boys and immature girls in the neighborhood of Templars' houses, and the street boys of London had a name for Templars that is not printed in a more fastidious age.

Most famous of all the enormities charged against them was the worship of the Golden Goat—he whose aureate hairs, found upon the mountain meadows, bring the shepherd luck. For the Golden Goat is none other than Pan, brought hither by the Greeks of old, Pan who multiplies the flocks and fills the shepherd's cradle, Pan whose worship still goes on, they say, as the cult of "Pandoise," in the village of Cabris, where on summer nights strange capers are cut under the thin guise of a Christian festival.

On that luckless thirteenth of October, 1307, when Philip the Fair of Face, Charles the Miserly, and the pope of Avignon, who did whatever he was asked, proclaimed in sealed letters that all Templars were to be seized, the Golden Goat appears to have been visiting Sir François de Boustan, commander of the castle at Pennafort high above the banks of the Loup. News of the contents of those letters leaked out before their time. Capture, Boustan knew, was certain; to be found with the Golden Goat in his possession would mean death with torture. And so he lifted the beast by its horns and flung it far over the cliff. But it did not die; it runs still, in the mountains, and may be heard but never seen, bleating in the lonely passes and the winter mists.

Of the commander of the house of St. Martin, above Vence, Hugolin de Capitou, it is related that he fled, but was captured and carried off to Tarascon, and prison. There all trace of him is lost in the silence that envelopes the end of the Templars. Under torture Jacques du Molay, Grand Commander, and one hundred and forty other knights, were made to say that they worshiped the Golden Goat and Baphomet, and to admit to crimes far more unnatural than these. When afterward they recanted, they were burned alive in Paris, and the voice of Du Molay was heard, through the flames, cursing the pope and the kings.

The innocence of the Templars, at least of the charges brought against them, has been established by modern scholarship. Their destruction had many fateful consequences. It hastened the conquests of the Turks, and obliterated the only international organization except the Church. More, their famous trial confirmed cruel criminal procedure in a way which lasted in France until the Revolution. The extreme veniality behind the accusations, the scandalous and unsupported nature of the testimony against them, the use of torture to obtain "confessions," left a black and lasting imprint upon European history. The mania for witch-hunting and burning at the stake received a tremendous impulse and sanction from the persecution of the Templars.

Most of the Templars of Vence had fled into Piedmont and were captured; some may have made their way to Portugal, where the king was doubtless glad to use them against the Moors. In Provence, when the king and pope were quite satisfied that no gold or jewels, nor evidence to prove guilt or innocence remained, the Templars' houses and forts were given to their old rivals, the Johannite Knights. This order, purer and finer, was to attract to its service the best blood in all Provence; there are ninety Villeneuves on its roster, and the greatest of all its commanders was Hélion de Villeneuve, hero of a hundred encounters. The Courmis family of St. Paul gave five sons to this service; the little town of Le Bar sent fifty-four knights. The village of St. Jeannet is said to take its name from the order.

But the great days of the Johannites (later, Knights of Malta) are yet to come; now they are settling into the Templars' magnificent quarters at La Gaude, that castle keep that watches both the snowy Alps and the sea. It is more doubtful if they ever occupied the Templars' great grim house at St. Martin. There is a vague superstition that this spot was accursed, and in the walls, it is said, were lately discovered skeletons of two girls of about thirteen and fourteen. These unfortunate children may not have been thrust there to conceal an orgy, but immured alive in the masonry. For there runs through medieval Europe the old folk belief that a fortress with a virgin sealed in its walls is impregnable. We have the old phrase, "a maiden fortress"; a maiden is said to have been buried alive under the Kremlin, and anyone who remembers the verses of "London Bridge" will suspect a secret darker than any child could guess.

But when at last there were no more floors to tear up in search of gold, and gossip about toads and goats and abducted maidens had died down, Vence settled back into the serious business of a good medieval community, which was domestic quarreling—in this case the great three-cornered struggle of bishop, baron, and burgesses.

CHRONOLOGY FOR CHAPTER FOUR

KINGS OF FRANCE

House of Capet

987	Hugh Capet
1031	Henry I
1060	Philip I
1108	Louis VI, the Fat
1137	Louis VII
1180	Philip Augustus
1223	Louis VIII, the Lion

1226	Louis IX, the Saint
1270	Philip III, the Bold
1285	Philip IV, the Fair

"Kings of Arles"

992	Guillaume II
1018	Bertrand I
1050	Geoffrey
1063	Bertrand II
1090	Gerbert. His daughter married to:

House of Barcelona

1112	Raymond Bérenger I
1144	Raymond Bérenger II, Count of Provence
1166	Alphonse I, King of Aragon, with Count Raymond Bérenger III, and his brother Sanche
1196	Alphonse II of Spain
1208	Raymond Bérenger IV. His daughter, Béatrix, married to:

House of Anjou

1245	Charles I of Anjou
1285	Charles II, the Miserly or the Lame

BISHOPS OF VENCE

1000	Arnoul
1025	Durand
1093	Pierre I
1114	Lambert
1155	Raimond I
1179	Guillaume I
1193	Pierre Grimaldi
1214	Raimond II

1222	Guillaume Ribotti
1263	Pierre III
1270	Guillaume de Sisteron

SEIGNEURS OF VENCE

(OF THE FAMILY DE VILLA NOVA OR DE VILLENEUVE)

1230	Roumiou (Romée) I	Enfeoffed by his Count, Raymond Bérenger, with the fief of Vence. Second son of Giraud, seigneur of Arcs and Trans *m.* Douce Bada
1251	Paul I (son)	*m.* Aicarde de Castellane
1293	Roumiou II (son)	Unmarried
1307	Pierre I (uncle)	*m.* Alasacie d'Aigunes

Chapter Five

THE MIDDLE AGES

FROM GOOD KING ROBERT TO
GOOD KING RENÉ

IN THE REIGN OF ROBERT THE GOOD, COUNT OF PRO-
vence and King of Naples, when a Saracen galley
slave was seneschal, and his wife, a washerwoman,
was governess to the king's granddaughters, Vence
boasted seven rival claimants to the seigneurie, so far
as I can make out, and it is permissible to suppose that
there were correspondingly forty-nine feuds. The
cathedral chapter too was in perpetual turmoil, struggling with the bishop over the payment of tithes, the
ownership of mills, or other unworthy causes. At

other times bishop and people were in unison. In 1323 there were riots in the Place Peyra, when the angry townspeople were harangued by Bishop Pierre VI into fury against the Villeneuves. Between bishop and baron the quarrel was purely pecuniary. Both masters sought support with promises of privileges granted and liberties renewed—promises that were never fulfilled. Vence sought justice of Robert the Good.

To pacify the uproar inside the dark constrictions of the walls of Vence, Robert sent as bishop (1333) Arnaud de Barcillon. The Seigneur François de Villeneuve wisely distracted attention from domestic hatreds by joining in the feud of the Guelphs and the Ghibellines. Vence and the Villeneuves were Guelph.

This is the era of the real beginning of civic liberty in Vence; the town was learning to play off bishop and baron and to appeal to the Crown, which was always anxious to extend the power of the towns at the expense of nobility and clergy. I do not know all the restrictions from which Vence then suffered; but the rights that she obtained sufficiently indicate what the lack of them must have been. In 1333 Vence asked and received permission to pierce window holes in her ramparts, provided they were grilled, and so for the first time in many a dark old room the blessed sunlight fell.

When Good King Robert died without male heir, he left his disparate possessions in the hands of an inexperienced, vain, and vivacious girl of eighteen, the tragic Queen Jeanne (or in Provençal, Jeanno; in Italian, Giovanna), Queen of Naples, Sicily, and Jerusalem and Countess of Provence and Fourcalquier, about whom innumerable legends cluster. Born in Florence (1327), granddaughter of Robert the Good, daughter of Prince Charles and Marie de Valois, her name is linked with romance and clouded with suggestions of dishonor. Her upbringing was in the hands of a coarse washerwoman who had somehow bewitched the Neapolitan court, and whose son is said to have encompassed the seduction of Jeanne even before her marriage at sixteen to the almost idiotic boy, Andrew, brother of King Louis of Hungary.

Proclaimed queen in 1343, she was pregnant with an heir when her husband was taken from her bed in Naples and hanged from the castle window. The conspirators will never be known, but Jeanne cannot quite be cleared of complicity. Her behavior was suspicious, her dislike of her husband too well known. The motive of the murder was hatred of the Hungarians who swaggered in Naples and incited Andrew, who was only a consort, to demand coronation. Her trial was begun at Rome by the famous tribune, Rienzi, but when Louis of Hungary advanced, bent on revenge, Jeanne had to flee, with her new husband, Louis of Tarentum, her cousin. She escaped to Provence, which she saw for the first time in 1348, when she landed at Nice in January of that year. Lest she had come to sell her Provençal estates (for her debts were notorious), she was suspiciously watched, and proceeded, almost a prisoner, to Grasse and finally to Aix. At Avignon she secretly sold the city to the worldly and genial pope there resident, for eighty thousand gold florins. Her trial for murder was marked by her brilliant defense in Latin, her excuse that she disliked her first husband owing to the influence of witchcraft, and by the speed with which the pope acquitted her.

Out of romantic fondness for this bright figure, the Provençal still speaks of her reign as the "time when things were as they ought to be," but ruthless history affirms that during her wardership the land was brought to ruin and civil war. The Black Death walked abroad, and the country was thick with robbers and brutal guerrillas called *armagnacs* and *écorcheurs*, and after them the *tard-venus* or "late-comers," who knew no law but pillage. The Jews were persecuted; there was a plague of grasshoppers; the Durance broke its banks. There runs an old rhyme:

> Mistral, Parliament, and Durance
> Have wrought the ruin of Provence.

In the mountains back of Vence the bold Arnaud de Servoules, who was called the "Archpriest" because the Avignon pope, Innocent VI, had tried to buy him off with the benefice of a parish, collected all the malcontents of the countryside and robbed, murdered, and pillaged. No mere highwayman was this Gascon, but a sacker of towns. On his account Avignon raised its walls higher. Queen Jeanne offered a fief to whoever would bring him to justice; Nice was in terror of him. It was Jean Siméon, bailiff of Vence, who finally defeated the "Archpriest" in 1358 at Brignolles as he was coming from the sack of Draguignan. For this Queen Jeanne made Siméon president of the *chambre rigoureuse* of the parliament of Aix.

When in 1348 Jeanne first saw Provence, it was as a woman that she appealed to her subjects. "I ask you only for your hearts," she said at Nice, and by the time she reached Grasse she had indeed won the hearts of Provence. She was fair and she was frail, and she was a woman who could, like Mary Stuart, put on armor or take off a stocking in a way to drive men mad for her. Wherever there is a weak woman, there will strong men be found. Jeanne's Provençal allies were Giraud and Paul de Villeneuve of Vence, René II of Monaco, Guichard de Villeneuve of Tourrettes, François de Barcillon of St. Paul, Rosso Rostang of Courmes, Honoré de Malvans, Blacas of Carros, and the two mighty counts of Tenda. All of them were eager to help her to win back the fatal throne under the shadow of Vesuvius, for hers was one of those sentimental causes that appealed to the medieval's sense of display and quixotry.

Aided by her Provençals she returned to Naples, having in her train Boccaccio and Petrarch. Her reign was now illustrious and peaceful, except that her husband's character had spoiled, and he knocked Jeanne about with his fists. In 1362 he died, and at once Jeanne took as a consort James III of Majorca, a king without a kingdom, who was permanently absent pursuing his crown in Spain and writing her for more money. When and where he died is uncertain.

Within two years the barons had discovered Jeanne's political and pecuniary double-dealings, and all Provence blazed with revolt. It was possible to grow very weary of Jeanne as well as to go mad about her.

In order to sustain her dubious finances, Jeanne went on selling off her Provençal estates. Thus her seneschal, possessing her permission to sell in her name, put up the fief of Vence, and it was bought in by the bishop and the Villeneuves as co-seigneurs. Uninformed of this sale, Jeanne sold it to the Grimaldis of Monaco. Though loyal to its queen, Vence nonetheless repudiated this second sale; the Villeneuves were its family; it would have none of the Grimaldis. Jeanne was obliged to revoke her sale.

But the Villeneuves were nothing grateful, and indeed they abolished the city's municipal council, that legislative and executive electoral body so hardly won out of feudalism. In the stead of the council the Villeneuves appointed bailiffs of their own choosing who had such powers as the right to collect taxes by force of arms and to arrest citizens in the name of the seigneurs.

In 1368 the Countess of Provence was again in her estates, granting charters to cities, granting letters patent and privileges. If ever Jeanne was in Vence it must have been at this time, and it is perfectly possible that the tower called Queen Jeanne's at the headwaters of the Malvans was then visited by her, though it was doubtless constructed earlier. The nearest authenticated habitation of Queen Jeanne was in Grasse, where she built a palace of which today only the kitchen stairs remain unchanged.

Still loyal to their fatal queen, Vence and her neighboring villages, her seigneurs and her people, took her part and that of Pope (or Anti-Pope) Clément of Avignon against Urban, the pope of Rome. But the Bishop of Vence, del Pozzo, a good Italian, was an Urbanite, and, fleeing to Gattières, he came out openly for the pope of Rome, though it lost him his see. Nice too was Urbanite, and the Governor of Nice in 1379 sent his army, under the mercenary captain, Spinola, against the mountain towns. The Villeneuves manned La Gaude, Gattières, Coursegoules, Gréolières, Vence, and Tourrettes. First the cruel Spinola attacked Gattières, was repulsed, and turned to Tourrettes. He found it defended by Guichard, a natural son of Paul the Seigneur of Vence, who flung down from the walls of his little town defiance against Spinola and the pope of Rome, and so stoutly did he defend himself that Spinola beat a retreat. By letters patent in that same year Jeanne made Guichard the seigneur of Tourrettes and the governor of the Var frontier.

After the death of James of Majorca, Jeanne married Otto of Brunswick, also throneless. Badly treated by the pope of Rome, Urban, she declared for Clément, the Avignon pope. Again she had to flee Naples, with the papacy, Hungary, and the great Neapolitan noble Charles of Durazzo all against her. She disinherited Durazzo, who was to have succeeded her, and left her crown to Louis of Anjou. In 1380 Naples seemed swinging back to her; she sailed from the Bay of Agay in the Estérels, to regain her throne. But Durazzo, infuriated, was still strong in Italy; and Louis of Anjou, regent of France, did nothing to rescue her when she was besieged by Durazzo in her castle at Naples. Provence too was not so ready this time to fly to the rescue. The galleys of Provence were her last hope after her husband was captured in the attempt to relieve her position; she scanned the sea despairingly for their sails. They arrived just four days after starvation had forced her to capitulate. On May 12, 1382, while at prayers, she was strangled by order of Durazzo. A generous, extravagant, amorous, untruthful, and lovable woman, "Good Queen Jeanne" is remembered in Provence as all that was fine and beautiful. Yet she was seldom in Provence, and thought of it chiefly as a tool for her Italian ambitions.[1]

So when the "singular pride of Italy" was done to death, the relentless Durazzo, her murderer and successor, was left nominal master of Provence, and sent his mercenary, Spinola, who sacked the land from the Var to Draguignan. Foulques d'Agoult,[2] the seneschal of Provence, howled for help, and the regent, Marie de Brétigny, came hastening, only to be blockaded by the "scourge of Provence," Count Raymond of Turenne.

When at last the regent and the seneschal had triumphed, Nice and Vence were delivered (1386), and two years later Vence, St. Paul, and Le Broc received letters patent from Marie confirming their municipal privileges. It was in 1387 that Nice, to extricate herself from a political stalemate, invited the Red Count of Savoy to take possession of the town. This meant that the County, or, later, the Kingdom of Savoy, now extended down from the Alps to the Mediterranean,

[1] Jeanne left no children; her infant daughters both died outside of Provence. But it is characteristic of the power of her name to attract legend that it is still believed at Roccasparviera, a phantom or abandoned village on the other side of the Var, that the screams of "her three murdered children" may be heard, and the vanished castle and village become again substantial.

[2] His daughter Bourguette he gave to the Seigneur Giraud of Vence to wife.

and the Var River thus became the boundary between Savoy and Provence. Vence, as being west of the Var, was left in Provence, but from this time on Nice and Vence were seldom on the same side in any war. Though Nice is the natural capital of the Riviera, an artificial boundary now split her province; Vence was to remain Provençal, and become French; Nice was to pass gradually from Provençal life toward a Savoyard and, later, an Italian influence. With the Var not half-a-dozen miles away, Vence found herself a small fortress on a dangerous frontier.

When after the death of Queen Jeanne loyalty no longer required that Vence take the part of the anti-popes of Avignon, the city and her little neighbors, her bishop and her baron, changed sides in the Great Schism, and in so doing followed their natural convictions. The move, however, was not so prudent as it appeared. Indeed it was daring, since the pope of Rome was far away, and the violent Anti-Pope Benoît XIII was close at hand, and stopped at nothing. In 1400 Vence joined with Grasse in repulsing the Genoese freebooters and assassins hired by the anti-pope to ravage the coast, driving them from Cannes; but they were unable to prevent them from sacking the abbey of the Lérins. For their pains the Vençois were excommunicated from the palace at Avignon.

In Good King René, Provence enjoyed at last another wise ruler. Toward the towns René was ever conciliatory, eager to win their favor against the barons. At the moment (1437) François de Villeneuve was at outs both with his townsfolk and with Bishop Louis de Glandèves, the bishop supporting the town in its struggle for a municipal organization peculiar to southern France. This was the council (like a board of aldermen) which had the right to pass laws and to elect two executives, the consuls, invested with the full majesty of the local law. These sought the right to walk on an equal footing with bishop and overlord, to wear silk, and to carry a sword.

The councils of Provence sprang out of the civic "universities," which were not institutions of learning but republics wherein the citizenry was universally embraced. It is astonishing what seemingly simple things the council of Vence had for three hundred years been demanding the right to do, or rather it is astonishing that it did not naturally possess such rights.

For instance, the council wished to man its own ramparts under its own military command; it desired to possess itself of the keys of the city and asked for the power to appoint the time, the place, and the tithes for markets and fairs; it claimed the right to spend its own tax money in the way it saw fit, and it wished to maintain police and construct waterworks. Vence even had to sue for permission to manufacture saltpeter. Every one of these demands and more were fought by the seigneurs.

To us the seigneurs' economic hold upon the community appears parasitic; their attitude seems carping and unreasonable. Probably the Villeneuves had the instinct common to the privileged that any change might be dangerous. Their refusal to admit even the consuls to equality in social and ritualistic details was as deep-seated as the antipathy of the country squire to placing a beggar on horseback or of an antebellum southerner to educating a Negro.

But justice demands that we remember that at the height of feudalism the whole feudal pyramid was economically sound enough in view of the peril to life and property in those times; it was at least a system that worked. Tradition insisted that the nobleman spend; it forbade him to earn. Small wonder that he looked upon any form of revenue from his fief as not only legitimate but indispensable.

The same extenuation must be held out to the Church for owning land, houses, mills, and farms, and for collecting tithes in highly secular places and ways. The temptation to take over economic and political power was forced on the Church in the crash of Roman civilization. The Church used these powers variously, but in general it strove to protect the poor and helpless.

But townsmen and farmers had begun to see that

96

they could form a political and economic bloc, based on communal reciprocity. Thus was the commune born. It grew in strength and daring; now it proposed to enlarge its advantages at the expense of the old seigneurial privileges, and though the temporal rights of the bishops were more leniently viewed, the sturdy hearts of the Vençois could be stony when the church really encroached.

So far did matters go in Vence in the days of François de Villeneuve that the Court at last had to intervene, and René, despite his inclinations, deemed it unwise to grant an outward victory to the commune against the powerful nobles. So he decreed that the consuls of Vence must go down on their knees, a lighted torch in their hands, and ask pardon of their seigneurs. But separately, and as if it had nothing to do with the case, René later confirmed the town in all its hard-won privileges, at the same time soothing the baronial vanity by reasserting the ancient hunting laws.

Many privileges still remained to the nobles and many irksome duties were still incumbent on the town. Thus fifty years later the seigneur in case of his capture in war could demand that the town ransom him; the town must furnish dowries for his daughters; and he had but to dip into the people's purse when a great company of knights came to visit him or a prince passed that way. Also there were special assessments if the baron married, if his wife was brought to bed of a child, or he wished to purchase a new fief. Should the baron plan a trip across the sea, or make votive offerings to a saint, it was, ultimately, the town that paid.

Despite these restrictions, this is an era of building and expansion for Vence. In 1430, François, the seigneur, built the "new" château that stands beside the Peyra gate. It wears still the dignity and early refinement of fifteenth-century architecture, though it is no self-conscious showplace. Only a few of its rooms are open to the visitor, who climbs the stairs to be rewarded with a cup of tea and a muffin in the English tearoom ensconced thus in *lo casteu*. A year after the castle was built, the town began to clear space for the *places* that relieve its crowded strictures. In 1440 were laid out the first streets outside the walls. When in 1450 the waters of the Lubiane were brought into the town, the Peyra fountain was erected (since restored). And here, I think, speaks the voice of Vence, running forever fresh and indomitable from some deep stony source, filling with the gush and sparkle of its story the quiet *place* under the château wall.

It is here, indeed, in the Place Peyra that the heart of Vence lies. Better to live outside the walls, where the sun falls and the flowers bloom, and there are villas quaint or opulent for the foreigner to lease. That is Vence, as the visitor may best enjoy it for a season or more. But Vence eternal lies under the shadow of the château wall, where the air is damp with ancient stone and tinged with the reek of wood smoke and baking bread and the very old taint of human living. Here, where once the seigneurs swaggered, the little shopkeepers do their business—the wine-seller and the baker and the widow in the black shawl who sells bright pottery. And here the women come to the fountain, as they have been coming for five hundred years, to fill their tall narrow pitchers at the clear, chill, spouting flow. Upon the thread of its musical running all the years seem to be strung, for in the Place Peyra the old and the new are coexistent, the ancient stone and the hot fresh loaf, the musty bottles at the back of the wineshop and the vintage still green in the cask. From the Peyra gateway it is not far to step back into the past. 55297

It was in the time of Good King René that Provence, and with it Vence, enjoyed the last, the golden sunset of her golden age. All that we think of, all that Europe even then fondly thought of as most characteristically Provençal—farandole, castle, troubadour, jongleur, hawk, hound, star-crossed lovers of noble families in feud, alchemists, astrologers, *damiettoes* (fairies) and *masques* (witches), and the Provençal speech itself (which, at its height of influence, extended from Catalonia in Spain to Piedmont in Italy) —all these, I say, were in their heyday between the reigns of Roumiou and René.

Those were the days when no one doubted that Pierre Nostradamus[3] could foretell all things when he donned his astrologer's cap. When no one doubted that in the village of St. Jeannet every man and woman and even children and cats were *masques*. When by St. John's Night fires lovers had their way. When festivals went on in all-night charivaris and dancing in the dew. When animals were blessed in church; when children married; when Pan kept the cradles full; when Good René was king.

It is not to be understood that when René died the Provençal culture and the half-legendary Provençal "feeling" went out of existence. Rather it declined slowly, and indeed it is not gone. At the Carnival of Flowers in Vence a few of the old costumes will be brought out (beside innumerable pretty modern imitations), and for brief hours the girls billow about the streets in red and white striped skirts, with tight-fitting bodice of coarse linen, delicate lace cap, and black straw hat, flat and large around as a cartwheel, hanging down the back.

And there are more intangible and more genuine survivals of the old Provençal spirit. There is the infrangible, modest, sunny courage of the people. There

[3] Grandfather of the more famous Michel Nostradamus (1503–66), the astrologer who cast horoscopes for the children of Catherine de Medici and Henry of Navarre, and who predicted that in 1915 the world would tremble with a war to be waged on land, in air, under the sea, and that three emperors would lose their thrones by it.

100

is the odd, fruity humor of the peasants, the tolerance, at once cynical and kindly. There is "dance, and Provençal song, and sunburnt mirth." And they have survived from the time of Good René, the king who never won a battle and never wounded a friend. The king who went about in an old black hat, disguised as a minstrel, and joined lustily in country dances.

I take the time of René as the sunset of Provençal glory merely because René himself was a bit of a revivalist; he talked about "keeping up the old customs." He sang forgotten songs and composed others in the old manner. He encouraged ancient dances and wrote a book on chivalry; he delighted in "Courts of Love," though they were going out of fashion.

Soon after René died, Provence lost its political identity and became one of the provinces of the French Crown. And at the same time the highly endemic quality of Provençal life was invaded and broadened by a greater culture, a spirit that had begun in Italy and was sweeping Europe—the Renaissance. Simultaneously Europe was feeling the effects of another influence, counteractive to the artistic grace, the worldly splendor, and the relaxing morality of the Renaissance. The Reformation was gathering its stern forces in the North. Vence was to spill good blood because of it, and, though in the end she returned to the olden faith, the age of innocence was over.

CHRONOLOGY FOR CHAPTER FIVE

KINGS OF FRANCE

House of Capet

1314 Louis X
1316 Philip V
1322 Charles IV

House of Valois

1328 Philip VI, the Fortunate
1350 John
1364 Charles V, the Wise
1380 Charles VI, the Well-loved
1422 Charles VII, the Victorious
1461 Louis XI

RULERS OF PROVENCE

House of Anjou

1309 Robert the Good
1343 Jeanne I
1382 Louis d'Anjou
1384 Louis II
1417 Louis III
1434 René the Good
1480 Jeanne II
1480 Charles III du Maine
1481 Provence passes to the French Crown, under Louis XI
     Transfer confirmed 1487

BISHOPS OF VENCE

1298 Pierre IV Malciati
1302 Foulques I
1312 Pierre V
1319 Raymond II
1319 Pierre VI
1326 Foulques II

1328 Raymond III
1333 Arnaud de Barcillon
1348 Jean I
1358 Guillaume III de Digne
1361 Étienne de Digne
1375 Boniface du Puy
1378 Jean II Abrahardi
1404 Raphaël del Mouzo (or de Monso)
1409 Jean III
1415 Paul de Cario
1420 Louis de Glandèves
1441 Antoine Salvanthi
1463 Raphaël II

SEIGNEURS OF VENCE

1309	Bertrand (son of Pierre I)	*m.* Béatrix d'Esclapon
1322	Truand (son), grand seneschal	*m.* (1) Dulceline de Pierrefeu, (2) Uranie de Villeneuve
1330	Roumiou III (son)	*m.* Alasie Marquesan
1338	Paul II (nephew of Bertrand)	Unmarried. His natural son Guichard founded the Tourrettes-Vence line
1341	François I (brother)	*m.* (1) Cécile d'Hyères, (2) Simone d'Esclapon
1369	Giraud (son)	*m.* (1) Bourguette d'Agoult, (2) Cathérine de Vintimille
1408	François II (son)	*m.* Sillette Riquier
1450	Hugues (son)	*m.* (1) Marie de Grimaldi, (2) Alix de Brancas
1456	Raynaud (son)	Unmarried
1458	Nicholas (half-brother)	*m.* Marguerite de Forbin

Chapter Six

RENAISSANCE

GLOOMILY OPENED THE SECOND HALF OF THE FIF-
teenth century for Vence. The plague was in the
land, and leprosy (which lingered in the dirty and
lawless town of Eze till *ca.* 1890). The consuls of
Vence and Tourrettes met in 1463 to take measures of
quarantine against the lepers. Meanwhile no measures seemed competent to deal with the plague; La
Gaude was so stricken that the population fled in horror from that place accursed to St. Jeannet. The
bodies lay unburied; men believed that the very soil
was deadly. So vivid was the memory of scenes of
horror and the suffocating fear of contamination that

for over one hundred years not a soul would go near the spot. Today it is again a little gray Provençal hill village that you may see upon your left as you go down toward Nice. The interruption in its history may account for the fact that, though it is an enchanting spring morning's walk to La Gaude, there is little to be seen when one gets there. It certainly explains why for many centuries La Gaude belonged to St. Jeannet. During the century of its desertion it was still a fief; its owners still paid taxes, father and son, though not one of them could have been persuaded to return.

Bishop Raphaël II of Vence, seeing eight thousand dead in Nice, and the hill towns choked with corpses and filled with the cries of the dying, took measures to protect his town. No stranger might come inside the walls, and the stricken were promptly removed outside. People who crossed to this side of the Var or the Loup were to suffer the *bastinado*. By these stern measures the prelate delivered his flock from the terror and dissolution of death, and Vence, miraculously spared, as it seemed to the inhabitants, in 1468 gratefully dedicated silver busts of her patrons, St. Lambert and St. Veranus.

When in 1470 the Black Death reappeared, again the gates were closed day and night, and though piteous refugees from the farms and other towns fled to Vence with ashen faces, begging to take shelter under the benediction of the two saints, the bishop seems to have been unwilling to lean too heavily on miracles, for the poor wretches were driven back at the point of the sword. And so while Grasse and Antibes were ravaged, Vence was spared this time, and again in 1474, by her relentless quarantine.

A happier time for Vence was the years from 1455 to 1459, when Jacquotin Bellot, native *imagier* of Grasse, carved the choir stalls of the cathedral. One hears so much of these, the chief artistic treasure of a town that is poor in treasures (owing to the rough usages of time, of war, and mold), that it is a disappointment when first one sees them. For the wood is very dark, and the lighting very poor, and the dust very deep. And if one has expected the deep chiseling, the fluid skill, the clarified grace of modern carving, as in the Thistle Room in Edinburgh or the choir stalls of the Cathedral of St. John in New York, one may turn away carelessly.

The figures are small, and there is not, I think, a single nose left on a face. The skill of Bellot was as primitive as it was vigorous. One can enter into the artistic mood of the choir stalls only if one thinks back to Italian primitives—the oblate faces, the lengthened limbs, the languishing abdomens and flat breasts of pre-Renaissance art. The wood was hard; the knife was blunt; the technical background of the artist meager. But as one turns up the seats, and digs

106

away the dust, peering in the bad light, while a woman with a key stands impatiently waiting for you to hurry down like the tourists, something vital, delicious, and historically significant begins to steal forth from the time-blackened little figures. Just as the *santons* or little plaster figures for the Christmas Nativity scenes convey in bright colors the spirit of Provence, so the choir stalls are a pageant, however dimly seen, of Vence in the fifteenth century.

Here are the butcher, the cobbler with his leather on his lap, the village scribe writing on his knee; a fat young peasant woman with coarse dress, and high boots on her stocky legs; a little maiden with a clear young face, her hair falling loose to her waist, a nosegay of flowers held primly in both hands under her little breasts. Here is a buffoon, showing his head between his thighs. Here is a lady with a chaplet. There a snake enters a priest's ear; a bat and an owl are superbly done. Provençal flowers, Provençal fruits, are everywhere. Canons in hoods file by, with psalters and hautboys. A monk is laughing, his lewd merriment still discernible. After all these centuries the jest still tickles him.

Indeed, there are some Rabelaisian touches. It must have been hard for some growing choir boy to sit attentive to a long sermon by the bishop, when a specimen of Bellot's wit enlivened the arm of his stall. No doubt he draped the sleeve of his little cassock deco-

107

rously across it, and prayed hard. But now the stalls are old and dim; I think the moderns who chant *Gloria*'s every Sabbath from the old loft are less likely to understand what it is they see than a fifteenth-century choir boy. If one asks how the artist could indulge such fantastic humor in a holy spot, one has but to remember that the Church was also the theater, the club, the cemetery, and the art museum of the Middle Ages.

People did not then tiptoe around churches, speaking in whispers. They stood up on benches and sang at the top of their lungs; people were not afraid to laugh in church; they were not afraid to dance, kiss, and weep. Beggars begged in churches, lovers loved in them, murderers murdered in them. And in the end the Church embraced body as well as soul within its peace; in one of the country chapels the odor of the bodies interred in the walls was intolerable. Fugitives spent the night in churches; animals wandered in as freely as in the barn where Jesus was born or were even led in for a blessing. People went to the church to get laurel leaves blessed that they might hang them above the door to keep out *masques;* they came to get amulets blessed to make their husbands more ardent. And the wise old Church duly arointed witches and did its best to recall straying husbands. The choir stalls of Vence were but expressions of a vivid age.

In those days, indeed, Vence shared, as much as a

poor and small mountain town could, in the pomp of
the Renaissance. The cathedral itself was enlarged in
the fifteenth century and, unfortunately, darkened by
the addition of a tier of benches. The building had
taken its essential form toward the end of the twelfth
century. Of the ninth-century church, stones and
tombs remain in the structure. The two still earlier
churches are represented by nothing but a few ornamented stones preserved in the ancient masonry.

The architects in 1480 were Jean de Brunetti and
Luc and Clément Ruppibus. All lived in Vence at the
city's cost, and probably also the "fountainist," Jean
Montanari, and the Italian painter Jacques Canavesi,
who came in 1491 from Ventimiglia to do canvases,
retables, and murals for Vence and her neighbors.
Settling in Vence, and marrying a Vençoise, he established a family. His son Antoine and his grandsons
François, Frédéric, Antoine, and Laurent were all
painters whose canvases are found at Le Bar, Vence,
St. Paul, Tourrettes, and Le Broc.

The needlework of the women of Vence, the sole
outlet for artistic women, also glorified the walls of
the church. Their tapestries depicted the life of St
Madeleine and of St. Gregory. Other tapestries
graced the *hôtel de ville*, the bishops' palace, and the
château. Each of these buildings possessed a library
during the Renaissance.

Music too was not neglected; it was the moment

when the purest spirit breathed over the music of the Church. Masters wrote for angelic effects from young boys' voices; and in 1505 the generosity of priests and townsmen established in Vence a school for boys to be trained for the choir and educated generally. It was the moment, too, of organs. Invention had perfected the different voices. Effects of incredible beauty ravished the astonished ears of the devout. To all this add the splendor of robes and lace, of embroidered altar cloths and sacred vessels studded with jewels, and you have the church of Vence (which was its theater and its real court life as well) at the zenith of its outward glory. When Bishop Aymar de Wesc marched in solemn processional, in the laces and embroideries from the needles of Vence women, with his chanting choir boys, with his miter glittering with pearls and diamonds and sapphires, the great cross of solid gold borne before him, the very brooches on his cloak of gold, the new organs rolling forth their thunders, then the hearts of the Vençois beat high, for it was their church; their money supported it, their workmen had built it, their women had ornamented it, their children's innocent voices, floating down from Bellot's carven stalls, reminded them of the angelic host.

Even outside the church the population and the churchmen gratified the Latin passion for pageant and processional, in making pilgrimages, through the meadows and over the hills, to every sacred spot, to every chapel where once a year a Mass was said. They never missed a noble wedding, even if distant, nor a funeral; but by daylight or torchlight, choir boys' voices mingling oddly with Saracenic dogskin tambour and wheedling Provençal flute, they threw themselves with the passion of children into this play that was their chief relief from the drudgery of life.

For the simple people of Vence, as for most of Europe, life was otherwise largely gray with obedience. The ancient structure of feudalism still stood, and only through cracks in it could they slip to the liberty one day to belong to them. Such a fissure now appeared in the bastion of seignorial power in little Vence. When Provence lost its political identity and passed to the Crown of France, the rights of the commune (carved out of the feudal despotism of the seigneurs), which the counts of Provence had granted, were all thrown into question under the new regime. The Villeneuves attempted to regain all their power by insisting that the writ of the counts of Provence no longer ran. The two co-seigneurs of Vence, Louis and Pierre, were minors; their mother was the proud lady Marguerite de Soliès-Pont, daughter of Palamède Forbin-Janson, first Royal Governor of Provence. Her brother, Louis Forbin-Janson, governed Vence for the two boys, and a pigheaded, iron-fisted regent he proved to be. The olive mill, built in 1501, which you may still see below the ramparts of Vence, in the little vale of the Lubiane, was a chief bone of contention. The seigneurs wished to force the population to grind all their olives at this mill, at any rate demanded. They desired also to shut down the mill whenever they saw fit, and claimed the right to lead the water of the Lubiane away in a canal, or store it in reservoirs of their own. From 1490 to 1556 Vence and the Villeneuves were in the toils of lawyers, struggling each for power.

So far did matters go that in 1410 there was fighting in the streets; angry mobs gathered with scythes and axes. The seigneur retaliated with armed bands. Heads were broken; houses were entered and the men dragged out to be clubbed. At last the Crown itself intervened, with the sharpest reprimand a Villeneuve had ever had to swallow, and the seigneurial party sent proxies to ask pardon of the proud consuls of the town, on bended knee.

The king's decision was that the consuls and citizens were not subject to do homage; that the fief was not subject to payment of tribute in silver nor in kind; that the commune should give three hundred and twenty-seven livres of *pension féodale;* that the mills were under the seigneurs but the citizens might use them or not, as they would; that the seigneurs were to raise no more mills; that the waters must not be held in cisterns. It was a popular victory, though it took a king to win it.

Almost it seemed as though the plague had waited for its old enemy Bishop Raphaël II (d. 1491) to depart. For in 1521 it appeared in Vence, St. Paul, Le Broc; and in their Château de Malvans ("Queen Jeanne's tower"), Jean and Raphaël de Malvans tossed in fever on their couches, near to death. Yet they lived—to die later in their appointed hour. And the plague removed itself, to keep, too, a later appointment.

Now the stage of Europe is preparing for two resplendent gentlemen of the Renaissance type, with all the Renaissance trappings of culture and display. Both were well educated, both crafty, both able to grasp, as the medieval mind had not been, the politics of Europe as a whole—handsome men, worldly men, patrons of art and science, professors of religion for state purposes, who lived like men that fear not God. Francis I of France and Charles V, King of Spain and Holy Roman Emperor, whose minions oppressed Holland and Mexico alike, were rivals. Besides holding in their hands interests politically opposed, they were temperamentally unlike and well suited to hate each other, though there was a Renaissance cynicism even in their enmity—they didn't quite believe it; they knew that their very hate was a gorgeous scarlet garment put on to please the crowd.

In Provence, to one who pores over them centuries later, the wars of Charles and Francis are rather monotonous and at the same time confused. For instance, the right arm of Charles and the most heartless oppressor of the French was the Constable of Bourbon, a Frenchman of blood royal, while Admiral Doria fought now on one side, now on another. In 1543 the Constable landed at Nice and began the ravishing of fair and innocent Provence. The French general, Montmorency, retreating on Marseille, burned the country behind him, that the invader might find a blackened land. Nevertheless, the Constable found plenty to burn, and plenty of peasants to butcher. His troops passed through Vence, which was too feeble to resist, and swept on to Grasse, and when Charles returned defeated, his soldiery revenged its feelings on the countryside.

The following year, after the capture of Francis at Pavia, the country was swarming with the soldiers of Charles, hostile as great ants. It was in these troublous times that Vence was edified by the presence of Bishop Cenalis, whose sermons were too long even for the patience of his clergy and who was called (I know not why) "the phoenix of bishops" and "the second St. Paul." Less learned than Paul of Tarsus, however, for he solemnly assured the readers of his poem "The Françiade" (of whom Ronsard was one) that all the French are descended from Noah. The phoenix of bishops spread his wings in 1530 and flew to another diocese. But, two years before he left, the

114

peste had come again, and Francis I was draining Vence of her men and money for fresh wars.

Yet when the test of war was put, Francis abandoned this frontier to the mercies of Savoy, which had taken the part of Charles and was always favorable to an excuse for a pillaging foray on the borders of Provence. Again in 1529 Charles invaded Provence. In the previous invasions the women had suffered at the hands of his mercenaries; this time they fared better; the invaders brought their own women —a great army of camp followers. The men whom His Most Catholic Majesty hired to do his butchering for him were blood-thirsty Spaniards, brutal Baltic Germans, Neapolitans with Vesuvian cruelty, the most lawless army in Europe since the Huns, and fresh from the sack of Rome, where an innocent population had been given up to the vilest butchery and outrage in its history, the barbarian captures not excepted. To these people the French abandoned the frontier of the Var.

Perhaps what Vence suffered strengthened her resolve to make resistance another time. For in 1536 the town prepared for siege as war loomed again. Food and ammunition were laid in store; the walls were strengthened and all gates but one closed up. Inside the walls cisterns were sunk, while outside the fortresses were reinforced—St. Raphaël in the commune of the Malvans, and the *bastide* of St. Laurent,

115

immemorial refuge on the brow of the cliffs. With Doria on the sea, Charles at the castle of Villeneuve-Loubet, and the Duke of Savoy already over the mountains, Vence seemed doomed, but owing to a fortunate swing in military tactics the town escaped.

Joyfully the frontier towns in 1538 heard that Charles and Francis were to forget the past and meet at Nice for peace. Francis stayed at Villeneuve-Loubet and Charles at Villefranche, with Pope Paul III hovering between them, a wise dove of peace. Vence had a good look at two of the most showy though certainly not the greatest men of the age. Behold then Francis, facile, fickle, feline. And Charles, iron-framed, iron-fisted, close-fisted, close-mouthed. And Pope Paul, born Antonio Piccolomini, known as Alexandre Farnese when a bishop and cardinal—did he lift up his eyes to the hills and behold and remember little gray Vence of which he had been absentee-bishop from 1508 to 1511?

Charles and Francis, despite fine speech at Nice, were at it again in 1543, and from October of that year until January of the next Vence was the host of a regiment of Scotch under the Earl of Lennox, who had taken service with France. The eyes of the Vençois must have bulged to behold kilts, but Vence was lucky to suffer nothing worse than bagpipes. At Nice, Francis allowed his ally, Kehyr-el-Din, the Turkish pirate, to carry off, as his spoil of the city

116

that had sided with Charles, fourteen hundred Christian souls.

But Francis is well remembered in the neighborhood. Not only did he found the convent of Passe-Preste at St. Paul but he gave the little town its fortifications that are its chief charm today. This, the work of the Arlesian engineer Mandon, was begun in 1556, and the traveler who wishes to behold a typical little hill town girt in defenses compact and picturesque, almost like a boy's seaside fort of sand, must go to St. Paul. There are the tortuous passageway, the fat-sided, cast-iron, snub-nosed cannon. There are the ramparts, and all the paraphernalia of one of those jolly sieges of boyhood where everyone was brave and nobody got hurt. But, say the Vençois, for all its lead-soldier militarism, St. Paul has never withstood a siege, while the ramparts of Vence, battered, obliterated on the south side, and less picture-book in the eye of the tourist, are rich in veritable derring-do.

In 1555 and for two years thereafter Vence wilted with the plague. Two years later the bishop joined the people in the Place Peyra for a protest against the usurpations of the seigneur. But these are mere leaves, blown before the advancing storm of the Reformation and its wars.

CHRONOLOGY FOR CHAPTER SIX

118

Chapter Seven

REFORMATION

Now, DEEP AS CONSCIENCE AND DISTURBING AS LIGHT
to a dreamer, Protestant thought moves beneath
Europe's event. It heaves the giant chessboard, tilt-
ing king and queen, castle, bishop, and knight. That
sunny southeastern square that is Provence feels the
universal unrest. Françoise de Villeneuve, in some
shadowy chamber of her château, filled with the
sound of the everlasting fountain in the court below,
opens a letter from the Count of Tenda, written in
this Year of Our Lord 1560. It warns her to keep a
sharp lookout for "bad congregations." By this the
devout count means Protestants, but the lady must

119

have crisped the letter with a scornful hand, for by this time she and her brave, fiery, and free-thinking husband Claude have themselves gone over to the Reformed faith. They have followed the example set by the apostasy of two of the bishops of Vence, Simiane and Louis Grimaldi de Beuil.

True that this change of heart at the château made trouble in the town. Claude de Villeneuve had been continually at outs with his fief. His bailiff's house was stoned and stormed. Seigneurial party and consular party came to blows in the streets, and then to assassinations in broad daylight. The conversion of the seigneur to the faith of Calvin at last quite alienated the town from its overlord.

For Provence, so long at home with saints and fairies, nursed on miracles and legends as pagan at their source as they were pious in their end, did not wholeheartedly take to this new way of thinking bred in the more rational North. Some there were who were indeed swept by conviction into the Reformed modes of worship. Others, especially the petty nobles like the De Grasse and De Malvans families, perhaps too the Villeneuves, were motivated by more secular intentions. They engaged, through Protestant affiliations, in a political gambit against the great nobles who were largely staunch in the Church. Some lesser citizens hoped that a religious revolution would effect a social revolution and that some sort of cancellation of the acts of the police or of creditors would ensue.

In its attitude toward Protestantism the Crown itself was vacillating and even ready to side with the Reformers against the powerful nobles, and this situation was complicated by the cross-currents of dynastic wars, when the favor of the Protestants might prove worth courting. In fifty years France had four kings, and none of them knew peace, and two died violently, and one changed his religion four times.

In the midst of these tempests, well might Vence waver; but there was a sufficient majority of Catholics within the town to close the gates against the Protestants. Those of the Reformed faith might meet outside the walls for prayer. But even the seigneur might not come in, and from St. Jeannet vainly demanded his revenues.

St. Jeannet itself saw the departure from the fold of many Protestant brethren, and Coursegoules in its bleak mountain fastness took up the sterner faith. At Tourrettes a Protestant preacher walked the streets bold as the Catholic curé. Gourdon upon its cliff sent down bands of singing warriors to join the master Protestant of them all, Pompey de Grasse, terror of the countryside. Paul de Malvans embraced the Reform, and the Sieur de Cannaux carried the sword against all cities adherent to the Catholic

121

League, aided by the dreaded Baron des Adrets, sacker of cities, mercenary, and religious weathercock.

In these fratricidal times Vence fell upon the most evil of all her days. Between the sentinels at her gate, alert for Protestants, stole in another enemy, the plague.

From 1579 to 1582 it raged, and panic descended on all men. The town saw whole families extinguished; people dropped suddenly in the streets; naked corpses were pitched from the doors. Any and all things might breathe contagion; one by one the shops were boarded up. Bishop Garidelli fled in terror to St. Paul, and in his absence crimes broke out; all law was at an end. Theft and murder went unpunished; the living snatched at every fleeting gratification.

Doctors attended patients in masks that completely covered the head and were provided with glass eyepieces and long birdlike beaks filled with spices, believed to be antiseptic; they wore only leather. Confessors dressed in blue, had themselves bled and purged daily, and washed their clothes in sulphur. The notary drawing a will at the bedside of the dying was himself stricken. The cathedral bell tolled incessantly, calling the people to kneel in the streets. Then death stayed the hand on the bell rope, and a silence fell more terrible than the clamor. When at last the plague moved on, like a good sixteenth-century community Vence took up her religious feuds where she dropped them from a stricken hand.

The Baron de Vins, for the League (which was as powerful as and more ruthless than the Crown and took orders only from the Guise family), recaptured every town but Grasse, under whose walls he died. Claude de Villeneuve, who as governor of Grasse had defended it for the Protestants, was allowed to march out with honors of war. To clinch the Catholic victory, the Duke of Savoy, Charles Emmanuel, came in the guise of champion of the Church, but in reality, by fishing in the troubled dynastic waters of France, to seize Provence for himself. Thinking of him only as a good Catholic, Vence, her bishop, and her chapter united in approving and abetting the Duke.

As Savoy moved on confidently toward Aix, there to take the crown of the Bérengers and the Angevines, he left behind for his cause the Duke of Mayenne. Vence, unaware of the conspiracy to wrest Provence from France, and loyal to the state religion, suspected no treason to the temporal rights of the King, and gave welcome to Mayenne.

But matters looked quite otherwise to King Henry IV, a former strong Protestant, a stronger dynast and firm patriot. The League and the Guises were his political enemies and they were traitors, Catholic or no Catholic. As for the move of Charles Emmanuel of Savoy, he saw it as piracy, and so in 1590 the King unchained his swiftest and most dreaded dog of war, the Dauphinois and Protestant Duc de Lesdiguières.

This daring old raider swept down upon Provence and, carrying all before him, sent Savoy flying. It must not be understood, however, that the King, in sending Lesdiguières, was launching an attack of Protestants against a Catholic people. He was seeking to punish Vence for siding with the Duke of Savoy—a foreign power. Lesdiguières, who happened to be a Protestant, was to Henry IV a mercenary of great resource. Probably the better part of his soldiers were Catholics; certainly many Provençals were Protestants.

While Lesdiguières was busy in western Provence, eastern Provence was first in the hands of one party, then of another. The Protestant captain, De Cannaux, in 1591 demanded the surrender of Vence. Receiving no answer, he battered a breach in her walls, carried off a big money indemnity, and passed on through St. Jeannet. In the spring of the following year Vence was in the hands of Savoy, with De Cannaux no further off than the Château of Malvans, and St. Paul and Coursegoules in Protestant hands. The violent Claude, Seigneur of Vence, was drowned, May 13, 1592, while fording the river Argens. "It was the judgment of Pharaoh," cried Bishop Leblanc. The new baron, Scipion, down at Cagnes, called on his rebellious fief to submit to him or he would summon Lesdiguières.

And on June 2, 1592, the invincible Lesdiguières

was at the gates of Vence. In his train was Scipion de Villeneuve, mocking the town that believed that two very dead old men of long ago could defend it. But the town, confident in its patrons, brought the silver busts of Veranus and Lambert to the walls, and grateful it was to old Bishop Raphaël II, plague-fighter, who had had them made.

Lesdiguières encamped upon the plateau of St. Michel, where now stand the convent and the public school. From this vantage he commanded the ramparts of Vence. "Aim straight at the bell tower, and may it fall at the first shot!" cried Villeneuve. Lesdiguières opened fire; the tiny garrison responded gallantly with its one cannon. The balls of the fierce old captain took no effect. He sent forward his shock troops, his scaling ladders, and his battering rams. But the ladders were hurled down. The Vençois poured down boiling lead, and dumped mountain rocks on the attackers. The "old fox of Dauphiné" saw the Vençois coming out for a sortie; he saw his undefeated troops defeated. He went into a rage; swearing, he ordered his army to waste no more time on a miserable little town that was not worth his powder. Leaving five hundred dead men outside the walls, sulky as an old bear he took his grumbling cannon over the Estérels. Vence stood at the peak of her military glory; her name resounded throughout France. Little David had killed his Goliath.

125

Would that there were no more to write of Vence in the religious wars. But the little town had strength for just one siege. When De Cannaux let loose on Vence the mercenaries under Gordon, Vence had to pour out her money to buy him off. But when the Duke of Savoy returned, the old fox being absent, the Leaguers trooped joyfully back. Vence began to perceive that whichever side won, she would suffer, but she had compromised herself deeply; there was nothing to do but to open her gates to Savoy now.

The light horse under Épernon, soldier to the king, appeared; the League in western Provence collapsed; Savoy fled; and Épernon was at Grasse. There was nothing for it but to ask peace, and Vence formally went over to the side of her king, and France. Bishop Leblanc had plunged deeply in the business; in his zeal for the Church he had opposed his king; it was from the safe distance of Nice, which Savoy held, that he began explaining and apologizing. The chapter too drew up a memorandum of excuses. It took several years and thousands of words to square it all.

In the meantime, following the sudden reaction toward the Crown amongst the *petite noblesse*, Scipion de Villeneuve went back to Catholicism, and he and his town were technically at peace. Even against those who remained Protestant there was less rancor. Religious toleration became a fashionable philosophy under Henry IV.

So Vence at last had weathered the storms, won glory, been sadly compromised, been humbled—and yet somehow had maneuvered herself into the position that she really wished to represent her, of loyalty to the Crown and France, yet steadfast faith in the Church.

Within the town itself there had been ecclesiastical troubles; Bishop Leblanc, though enthusiastically admired by many Vençois, had enemies too, and unfortunately the bishoprics of Vence and Grasse had been united as a result of his endeavors—a measure financially advantageous to a bishop, since both sees put together were still very poor in comparison with a fat living in Normandy or Champagne. But it was infinitely distasteful to the proud Vençois. Had they not given to the world two saints and a pope, and been a buckler of the Church? They would have none of Grasse, and some of the best names in Vence are consequently found in nothing less than a conspiracy to take the life of their bishop.

A choir boy on the Sunday of May 20, 1596, idly ran his finger over the back of the bishop's seat. Suddenly a board gave way; he put in his hand; under the episcopal throne he felt something strange, and drew it forth. Enough gunpowder was found to blow up the choir stalls of Bellot, to blow up the whole chapter, to blow up the cathedral. Word was passed to the bishop, but he calmly finished his sermon.

But the tale runs out ahead of itself. Alas for Vence, her military adventures were not over; as she was now French, in 1595 her position was cruelly exposed to the Leaguers and to Savoy, who were not likely to be tender with her for changing sides. There were still four sides to take—the die-hard Protestants', the King's, the Leaguers' (whose religious significance is almost lost in antiroyalism), and Savoy's. The last two worked together for predatory purpose. Vence chose the side of the king—and the League and Savoy swept down upon her. The king sent Épernon to steady the Vençois' loyalty; he had to be furnished with ruinous quantities of supplies and money.

Vence saw trouble brewing, strengthened her fortifications, borrowed money, and bought up a supply of wheat. The plague came. Captain Esprit de la Plaine came, and was as bombastic as his name; he listened only when money talked. The Sieur de Cannaux came (1597) and was bought off with the last sou in the town's treasury—a borrowed sou at that.

When in 1598 the Edict of Nantes laid the dust of the religious wars, and most of the country around returned voluntarily to the old Church, Vence found herself with the enormous debt of one hundred thousand livres, and commerce and agriculture in such a ruined state that the taxes were impossible to collect. The poor, without homes or work, made up bands of robbers who drifted about the country, stealing the farmwife's butter and the shepherd's lamb, and dwelling by stealth in abandoned houses.

In 1601 Leblanc left the see of Grasse-Vence for Aix, where he died. He was remembered fondly in Vence even though they had once tried to send him to Paradise with gunpowder. Every year at the feast of St. Veranus it had been his custom to dower a needy girl of the commune. Coming rich to the old town, he left poor, his substance spent in charity.

Though the Villeneuves of St. Jeannet and Tourrettes "remained in the error of their way," the Reformed faith in Vence expired like a short candle. There is something in the nature of the Provençal that is not protestant. The Provençals were contented with their religion. Why not, since they had made it? They had inherited the Mediterranean tradition of local nymphs and sacred grottoes. They supplanted them with local saints and holy places. They thought the faith of Luther and Calvin too barren; its God seemed too vengeful, its Devil too dangerous. Provence must have been glad to get back into rapport with a God who loved the expression of art and ardor and merriment in religion. It may even have been glad to see its old friend the Devil again, a Provençal Devil, who knew them all well, and had studied their tastes and habits from childhood to the grave.

CHRONOLOGY FOR CHAPTERS SEVEN
AND EIGHT

130

Chapter Eight

ANTOINE GODEAU

FROM THE DUST OF THE WARS AND RELIGIOUS HATES
Vence picked herself up and began to bind her wounds.
First she struggled bravely with her staggering debt
and slowly accomplished its liquidation. In 1603 the
separation of the sees of Vence and Grasse was again
acknowledged; their union by bishop and king had
never received final papal sanction. Thus the pious and
gentle Pierre du Vair was Bishop of Vence only. To
him Vence owes the chapel of Notre Dame de l'Arat,
built in 1610, and the chapel of the Pénitents Blancs,
commenced in 1614.

In our day it is only once a year that Mass is celebrated in the chapel of the White Penitents, because the order is extinct. But up to the middle of the nineteenth century nothing was more characteristic of the common folk of Vence than its love of these so-called penitential orders. They had their origin in the maniacal asceticism, imported from early Syrian and Egyptian Christianity, which marked the Church in Provence during its first centuries. There was a fanatical order of flagellants established at the mouth of the Var in the fifth century. As time went on and these orders turned toward socially useful and popular institutions, the flagellation diminished and soon became extinct.

The social evolution of the orders was toward fraternal societies of the laity, sponsored by the Church. Their counterpart today is found in the Masonic Temple; their counterpart in the Roman world will be traced to the trade guilds (though not at all to the medieval trade guilds). In short, they were mutual insurance and burial fund associations, social clubs for men, with costumes, offices of dignity, and initiation ceremonies; they served such useful public functions as the burial of the dead, the nursing of the sick, protection of strangers, and they offered such pleasures as the ringing of the bells on feast days and the setting-off of fireworks. In fact, the Penitents took over most of the showy lay offices of the Church, whether gay or sad. Above all, the Penitents delighted to make

132

processions and pilgrimages in costume, with singing and the waving of banners.

The most ancient of these orders as a popular institution was the Pénitents Blancs of Grasse, founded in 1186. In Vence and St. Jeannet the order was founded in 1566; it soon became rich by legacy and was practically the chief outlet for the play instinct of a histrionic people. When in 1614 the Pénitents Noirs were established in Vence, they were probably recruited from the ranks of the persons who had not been included in the more exclusive, older White Penitents. Also the Black Penitents found little left to them but the lugubrious duties of the community.

In Vence, but not in Vence alone, their rivalry was sometimes bitter; it was, indeed, one of the chief emotional pleasures of belonging to one of the orders, and in the end the rivalry resulted in a conflict that brought about their suppression, though the rise of national, commercial insurance companies probably explains their economic decay. At any rate, in the nineteenth century the Black Penitents of Vence and the White Penitents, while making processions, met in a narrow place and began to push each other off the road; presently crosses were cracking over Penitent skulls and *Te Deum*'s changed to battle cries. The same thing was to happen on May 31, 1821, when the White Penitents of La Gaude got in the way of the White Penitents of St. Laurent la Bastide, while their confreres of St. Jeannet looked on, cheering each side impersonally. Today these orders mount no more through lavender and thyme on St. Veranus' Day to the summit of the *baou* in chanting procession symbolic of the flight of the Vençois from the Saracens, as the Passover symbolizes the flight from Egypt.

But I must return to the goodly Pierre du Vair, who stood with the townsfolk against the Seigneur of Vence when he sought to impose fresh taxations. Scipion de Villeneuve called to his aid his clan; on his side he had the king's prosecutor. But the town appealed to Louis XIII, and he restored its olden liberties, its town hall, and its council that had been lost in the shuffle of the wars. Bishop du Vair loved the little old city as a spouse. "My wife is poor," he said, "but I will not quit her for a richer one."

It is from the hand of Du Vair that we have a document warning folk against the *loup-garou* or werewolf who seems to have made free with human flesh in those days. In olden Provence one had to be on one's guard against such enemies, and the trouble was that anybody might be a werewolf or a *masque*. But men or boys whose eyebrows met and who were encountered after dark were especially likely to be werewolves, and along the river Loup the benighted stranger often met Corybantic washerwomen, who, luring him by a rigadoon, encompassed his death.

It was in 1634 that a terror whose origin seemed to

the Vençois as supernatural as werewolves appeared again in the land. The bubonic plague was once more abroad; Digne had been reduced from eleven thousand souls to five thousand. But Vence was miraculously spared, and once again popular belief ascribed this delivery to the protection of the patron saints of Vence. While Nice was stricken and awaited the arrival of the bones of a saint of Sicily which were reputed plague-scarers, many of her citizens fled terror-stricken to Vence. Among the refugees was a senator of Nice, Honoré Leotardi, who hid himself in the fortress-village of St. Laurent la Bastide, refuge in all dangers. Here, it is said, he wrote that hymn to St. Lambert that two years later was sung by one hundred and fifty pilgrims from Bauduen, birthplace of Pierre du Vair and of St. Lambert, come to beg relics of the saint to drive away the plague. Around the walls of Vence they marched, accompanied by one hundred and fifty musketmen, the bishop, the clergy, canons, choir boys, all chanting the sweet invocation to the long-dead holy man, and at the tail of the procession marched the town musicians of Vence "playing very softly on fife and tambour." It was the last notable act in the life of the old bishop. He died in that same year, a luckless year of great drought, a foreboding year when a comet blazed prophecy nightly in the heavens.

It is said that, in dying, Du Vair expressed the wish that Antoine Godeau, brilliant young Academician

135

then in Paris, should take his place. Certain it is that in 1636 that darling of the *salonnières* was posting along the road toward Grasse. Once again the bishopric of Vence was united to Grasse, this time by the worldly prudence of Cardinal de Richelieu, who knew that there was not a proper living to be had out of either diocese separately.

The Grassois, going out to welcome their new prelate, were disappointed (though they politely concealed it under showers of orange blossoms and roses, and well-simulated cheers) to find that their bishop, already a famous man, was only a very young man, a very short man, and oh, such a homely little fellow. "*La figura d'una singe!*" they whispered. A monkey face, the skin wrinkled and brown as old wood, the nose and upper lip curled into the expression of one who does not like a smell. And his manner was diffident, uncertain; the affable Grassois continually felt embarrassed for him. They could understand an ascetic bishop or a worldly bishop; but an ugly little bishop who was a poet and the pet of those great ladies in Paris—no, it was hard to be at ease with him.

And uneasy was his diocese. It was composed of fifty-two parishes of which fully one-third were chiefly perpendicular, considered inaccessible to a bishop, and practically heathen ground; in another third Godeau was invited in clear accents to stay away. For the people of Vence refused, in defiance of the king and the terrible cardinal, to recognize the junction of their see to Grasse. Though they faithfully forwarded their ecclesiastical revenue to Godeau, though they respected his fame and were bitterly jealous of the Grassois in the possession of so distinguished a man, they never asked Godeau to visit their church or preach a sermon to them.

Godeau was not unused to rebuffs, despite his success. In his youth, as a student in Dreux (his birthplace), he had persistently inscribed verses to a young lady "of good family and pretty figure, but poor." While he sued anonymously, the girl's parents bestowed her hand elsewhere. The verses decorously ceased. But almost at once the lady was widowed, and presently the verses were renewed. The widow, who was to become known as "the fickle lady of Dreux," made it publicly understood that she would like to meet their author, and, the word having reached Godeau, he came to call. The young woman could not conceal her disappointment and distaste. Godeau saw that look, and fled to Paris.

There he lodged with a young writer friend, Conrart, and became a member of one of those little groups of serious thinkers that feel the burdens of the world and settle all its questions—and occasionally produce an Aristotle, a Shelley, or a Godeau. Some of the other boys (they were little better) were Chapelain, Balzac, and Boisrobert, a friend of Cardinal

Richelieu's. So it happened that the Cardinal came to bestow a paralyzing blessing upon the group; he wrote and asked them if they would not like to form themselves into a body, and meet under public authority. Thus was founded the Académie Française, of which Godeau was one of the forty charter members. Gone were the cozy little meetings; gone the young spontaneity, the free speech and thought. Henceforth their words must be recorded, their speech must be measured; they have a tradition to uphold, literally stately.

But enjoyment blossomed in the society of the *grandes salonnières* who held sway in drawing-rooms both in Paris and in country seats. These were an analogue of the "Courts of Love," where refined manners, beautiful garments, coterie speech, and match-making were all blended in that patronage of the arts so dear to the woman of leisure in all ages. The very capital of this fanciful world was the Hôtel Rambouillet in Paris, later the target of the young Molière in the satire that first made him famous, *Les Précieuses ridicules*. The leading ladies of the Rambouillet circle in Godeau's time were Madame de Loge, Angélique Paulet (named "the lioness" on account of her tawny mane), and Julie d'Angennes ("the princess"). The little poet was soon known as "Julie's dwarf," so much was he the pet of the salon, and his love poems were on all the ladies' lips. From

138

court subjects he progressed to paraphrasing a large part of the Bible—including the Epistles of St. Paul—in Alexandrine couplets!

The view which his contemporaries took of Godeau's verses was ecstatic, although it seems to us almost incredible that anyone ever took pleasure in plowing through fifteen thousand stanzas imitated from Ovid, on *The Annals of the Church*. No one now, I think, would call Godeau a great poet; his verse is frequently platitudinous and oftener overembroidered with imagery; the reader need not travel far before encountering a roseate wing, a gentle zephyr, or a gilded lily.

Then in 1636 "Julie's dwarf," the pet of the ladies —successful with none—entered the priesthood. He hoped to attain in due time, no doubt, some commendatory abbacy—that is, the sinecure of an absentee-abbot who could live in Paris while drawing the revenue of some fat churchly fief. Diplomatically, he had dedicated to the great Cardinal a poetic paraphrase of the psalm "Benedicite omnia opera Domine."

In his palace the Man in the Red Robe put down the poem and took up the map of France. Where should he place this new pawn of the Church, only eight days a priest but a nine-day wonder in the world of letters? A pun—both neat and becoming a prince of the Church—gleams in his devious mind, and drawing pen and paper toward him, he inscribes it:

139

"Monsieur l'abbé, vous me donnez Benedicite: je vous donne Grasse."

Godeau was aghast. "Grasse? But where is Grasse?" The *salonnières*, the Academicians, piece together what little they have heard of it. It is the farthest, the poorest, the stoniest, the most unruly diocese in the whole of the dominion. Not a handful of the congregation will understand one word of French, much less the turn of an Alexandrine couplet.

Godeau declined, reconsidered, reluctantly accepted. The abbot-commendatory of the Lérins could live in Paris, but a bishop is obliged to find himself in his cathedral on certain days—at Easter, at Christmas, Trinity, Ascension, Assumption. There was nothing for it now but to go. Farewell to Rambouillet. Farewell to great ladies, who flattered the beautiful mind behind the ugly face. "I expect to find more thorns than orange blossoms," said Godeau to Chapelain. Then the door of the post chaise slammed. Paris was gone.

For sixteen years Godeau occupied the episcopal palace at Grasse, and bit by bit became by sincerest conversion a lover of Provence and its comely people, of its naïve faith and its gay airs and its hills rich in tradition of martyr, saint, and bishop.

In the study of his palace he taught himself Italian and was ravished by Dante, Tasso, and Petrarch, and he wrote, wrote, wrote. Histories of the Church, in

140

prose and verse; verse paraphrases of the Bible; tracts against heresy; letters to his platonic friend "Julie" (now Madame de Montausier) and to Conrart, Chapelain, and the Hôtel Rambouillet.

"How can the oreads of your rocks, the nymphs of your valleys, the nereids of your Mediterranean, keep you in such a country?" asked Chapelain. Godeau replied with a verse from Job: "I will die in my nest." But Rambouillet never gave up expecting his return. Surely he would tire of the rustic pose. Surely fate would rescue from provincial ennui their pride. Surely he would have eaten enough of the lotus. He returned indeed to Paris, for brief visits, and was hailed like a missionary come home from Cathay. But always he hastened back to his cure of souls.

I do not know when Godeau first saw his church at Vence. In 1642, asserts Doublet, his careful biographer, he was there for at least the third time. On one visit he was stoned in the streets; Tisserand asserts that on another occasion a citizen named Guérin fired a shot at him from an arquebus, and that the gentle prelate would take no action against his attacker, but allowed him to exile himself.

When in 1644 arrived the bulls announcing papal sanction of the union of Vence and Grasse, Godeau deputed the Abbé Falconi of La Gaude, and Claude Barcillon, Seigneur de Malvans, to take possession of the church of Vence in his name. Asked for aid, Gaspard de Villeneuve, Baron of Vence, replied that he did not mix himself up in affairs of the Church. The sacristan would not proceed with the installation. The sub-sacristan did not know where the keys to the church were; under threat of five hundred livres amende his memory improved. The *abbé* and the noble proceeded to the altar, read the bulls to empty pews, and retired. At once the chapter rushed into meeting and drew up a protest to the throne.

Up to this time Godeau had been a shrewd politician in the temporal matters of his church, tireless and almost grasping in enlarging his diocesan benefices. He had journeyed to Turin in order to demand, in vain, from the Kingdom of Savoy the parish of Gattières (which, though it lay on the west bank of the Var, had been ceded to Savoy and fallen like spoils to the bishopric of Nice, so that for the bishops of Vence this enclave was as a thorn in their sides). But now, when the Vatican had at last confirmed the union of Vence with Grasse, and his revenues for the first time were brought up to something like a decent living, Godeau himself had a humble change of heart. He saw that if Vence would not come to him, he must go to Vence. He had become too sincere a churchman to put his pride ahead of the spiritual needs of his rebellious parishes. They must not stand insurgent against bishop, king, and pope. So he asked for the disunion of the two dioceses and for his transfer to the smaller, poorer town. Vence had turned a cold shoulder to him; to win her he must give her a complete devotion.

Godeau chose carefully the moment of his entry into Vence—May 26, 1654, St. Lambert's Day. He found Vence a town already obsolete in its aspect and its importance. In the Middle Ages when Provence was at its apogee, thick-sprinkled with castles and keeps, and all towns were small, a city like Vence was little smaller and less important than Nice; many an Italian city of that size called itself a state, made treaties, defied popes. Vence was once no more incommodious or unhealthy than Paris, since even kings then lived in inconceivable dirt and discomfort. But commerce, the great civilizer, in Godeau's time had not touched the Nice Provence, and the cities remained small, as crabbed and backward as in the time of Queen Jeanne.

The *petite noblesse* of the region was now less wealthy, actually or proportionately, than of old, and certainly less powerful and less necessary in the social structure. Vence had lost self-confidence; it knew itself rustic in the eyes of Paris.

To visualize it as then it was, one must now go to a point on the St. Jeannet road and look at its north exposure across the little vale of the Lubiane. Just so Godeau must have beheld the ramparts, the leaning gray roofs, the plain, manly bell tower, and *lo casteu*,

the château at the west gate. Save for the new municipal building, with its cluster of telephone wires converging over its roof, little of Vence-within-the-walls
is different today when seen from the north. The
south wall is now obliterated and unattractive save for
its old gates.

Godeau found that the fine old bell tower was half
in ruins and uncleanly as any stable; he learned that
every time the mistral blew, the bells, on their worm-
eaten struts and beams, were in danger of being blown
to the pavement. God, he told the Vençois, sent the
wind as a penitential scourge, yet he so far interfered
with the operations of Providence that he caused the
bell-ringers to sleep in the tower, to hold the bells in
place in case God's ire threatened to unhinge them.

The episcopal palace, which you may still see arch-
ing the street between the church and the municipal
building, he found to be a gaunt, gloomy old ruin, but
he soon had it filled with his books and tapestries from
one of which looked down the figure of Abraham.
Many a poem and essay written there was read and
recited throughout France. Conrart envisioned his old
friend's life in Vence as an idyll, and wrote him thus:

> Deep in the month of December,
> In your hall or in your chamber
> That looks upon the orangeries
> Perfuming all your orchard trees
> Whose leaves, through winter, green abide,
> You dine—the casement open wide—

144

And breathe of airs that softer blow
Than those that we in May can know.[1]

Godeau wrote, sighing: "I should be perfectly happy if fewer leagues divided me from Rambouillet." And in verse his wistfulness speaks out:

O Rambouillet! O nymphe si jolie
Souffrirez-vous que je sois confiné
Dans ce désert?

Surely Godeau must have known nostalgia, at times, pacing the garden he had laid out, just beyond the Peyra gate. What, alas, is become of his flowery plots? If the traveler asks himself why a dusty square without one blossom in it bears the name of the Place du Grand Jardin, let him remember the little bishop's garden, and think that the trampling feet of the Revolution beat it as flat and as barren as that hyperbolic desert in which, in perplexed moments, Godeau complained he was confined.

For there is no denying that there were aspects of his duties and sides of life in Vence that might have proved distasteful to a less fastidious man. If the countryside was enchantment, the slums of the town

[1] The translation is mine; the lovely original reads:

"Au milieu de mois de décembre
Dans votre salle ou votre chambre,
A l'aspect de mille orangers
Qui parfument touts vos vergers
Et dont la feuille est toujours verte,
Vous dinez, la fenêtre ouverte,
Et respirez un air plus doux
Que celui de mai n'est pour nous."

145

were depressing. Nothing distressed Godeau more than the choir boys' school, yet he was able to accomplish almost nothing toward improving it. One of his successors found that the few boys who attended it slept all in one big dirty bed, that they spent their time in smoking and playing cards, swore like soldiers, were illiterate and utterly ignorant of music, and were allowed to roam the town, on the quest of sweetmeats in the shops and *gamines* in the alleys. Godeau gave his private fortune to the founding in Vence (1657) of a theological school called "Les Pères de la Doctrine Chrétienne." It is commemorated today only by the Rue du Séminaire.

Humbly Godeau began at the fundamentals, and applied himself to learn the ways of his cure of souls. With utmost zeal he took up Provençal. His listeners heard with sympathy and an admiration that succeeded to amusement, his struggles, finally triumphant, to preach in patois. So, little by little, the pride of Rambouillet, the poet who found it so easy to talk and easier still to cover paper with ink, was wearing off; the savant-in-priest's-clothing was become a simple man before God and his fellows.

The diocese of Vence was small of extent and, in its flowery, sloping southern half, easy of access. But in its mountainous northern half, that stretched away to the Cheiron Range and the boundaries of Savoy, were only desolate rock plateaus, sparsely inhabited by a rude and ignorant people who lived for much of the year in the mists. To many communities no road led; a goat track must be followed afoot.

Here if anywhere one could credit the prevalent belief in *masques* and the *loup-garou*. Here, over the white stones, over the lavender and the whistling grass, over the ruins of a Templars' house with its haunting dark memories, the north wind blew with all its might, and sometimes the saint of a shrine was flung down on its face as if evil spirits still held sway there.

The bishop on his rounds sometimes discovered in these mountain parishes that a country priest was drowning his loneliness in drink or in joining in those rustic saturnalia which echoed pagan times. Cybele was still unconsciously acknowledged in dances commingled of Greek and Moorish elements. Godeau was offended by the gestures of the wild rigadoon, but fulminated vainly against it. Probably his parishioners did not allow Monsieur *l'évêque* to witness the *restroupado* in which the skirts of the girls were raised to the *demi-cuisse*, still less the *fougnarello* or the *pesouiouso* in which one by one the garments of the dancers were flung away, "jusqua ce qu'on restat en chemise."

Strange were the usages of devotion in Provençal parishes in those times. There is a record that in one country chapel the altar cloth was a woman's petticoat trimmed with green and black passementerie and

147

imitation silver. In another, one hears of complaint that the rats ate the Host, and the priest, to stop the wind that shrieked through the unglazed window, stuffed his cassock in the aperture, shutting off light and wind together.

The church of St. Paul, complained Godeau, had such a quantity of rancid oil stored in its crypt that it attracted vermin. At Le Broc manure was piled against the door of the chapel. Though at Bézaudun the people welcomed their bishop with the traditional salvo of drums, the prelate bewailed the indifference to the most ordinary conventions of decency in worship. It was nothing extraordinary for the young bucks of a Provençal congregation to fire off pistols at the elevation of the Host—not through disrespect but by reason of native enthusiasm.

Yet no parish was too distant for Godeau. In 1670, old and in ill-health, Godeau climbed up to the cliff village of Courmes, considered by all his predecessors inaccessible. On a December night, in ice and snow, he arrived, and the next morning said Mass in the chapel that from September to May was closed and without a priest. Seventeen families came through the drifts—the whole population of Courmes. When the priest was absent in winter, learned Godeau, there was no one to perform baptisms or funerals. Both the bodies of the dead and the newborn were carried across the treeless rock plateaus to Coursegoules. In the exposure this entailed many of the babies died before baptism.

Had Godeau come in summer he would have seen a spectacle in its way as shocking to a rational religionist. Here, it is said, St. Arnoux in 601 had taken up abode in a grotto beside the roaring Loup, under the pines and oaks and hornbeams, and in later years a chapel had been erected on the spot. Now people believed that those who bathed in the pool at the foot of the fall were cleansed of their sins, and thousands of pilgrims toiled up to this spot, and with lighted tapers marched nine times around the chapel, said nine *Ave's* and nine *Pater noster's*, confessed to the ear of the priest in the chapel, and then threw off their clothes, slid down a rock into the pool, and bathed. Afterward they retired to the woods to eat, sleep, and make love.

Long had the bishops of Vence waged war against this tawdry spot of pilgrimage. When the local priests were forbidden to hear confession in the chapel, the bishops of Grasse, hereditary foes of Vence, set up a confessional (and sold the indulgences) on the other side of the Loup, which was in their diocese.

When the summer heats lay enervating and blinding on Provence, Godeau was wont to retire to the little summer palace at Le Broc, coolest of the parishes, where he could gaze up the valley at the snows of the Italian Alps, and catch their refreshing breath.

The door of the bishop's house still bears the arms of the Academician. But in winter Godeau was generally to be found in the episcopal palace at Vence. In his old study, where Abraham looked down from the tapestries, nothing could be heard but Godeau's pen, covering quires of paper with letters to Rambouillet and interminable poems. Under the arches beneath the palace we see the folk of Vence plod through the winter mud, the winter mists. A girl going to the Peyra fountain with buckets; old women bent like the lonely ilex trees on the stone plains; children plump as dumplings toddling over the cobbles. A wave of sheep and goats, driven in to market, flows under the palace. We can imagine the last of them, an old goat, who looks up at the spire of orange where the bishop's candle burns beside his manuscript. He bleats at the right reverend writer of Alexandrines, and rubs off a golden hair against the pillars. The rest of the flock has gone on—the way of all sheep. The old goat makes a sound like laughing, drops behind, trots unnoticed out of the city gate, and escapes.

Godeau must have turned sometimes from his poems, in those long evenings of 1659, to polish off the sermon he was to preach in the chapel of the Oratory at Aix, in the presence of Louis XIV, Anne of Austria, Mazarin, the Prince of Condé, and the court. His subject was a sure one—"The Greatness of Jesus"—and he preached it brilliantly. Once again the great of France see the earnest homely brown face of the Academician, listen to his perfect periods, and remember the name of Vence.

But that was a worldly interlude; the days found Godeau usually in the midst of his people, tireless in their service, and so he went his rounds for many a year, until on March 28, 1672, the sands ran out. While chanting the *Tenebrae* in Holy Week, as one by one the candles were extinguished, Godeau felt a sudden paralyzing chill. As the last candle was snuffed out, the figure in the robes dropped to the floor. They carried him to his palace, and laid him in his unbleached linen sheets. He breathed a few hours more; then Abraham gathered him into his bosom. *Nunc dimittis.*

Chapter Nine

KINGS AND QUARRELS

NOW I LIFT MY HEAD FROM THE HEAVY VOLUMES, THE small type, the minutiae of detail in my source books. Ahead of me lies the part of my story which is closest to the present. Essentially it is modern history, almost as rich in names and places, as precise in dates and statistics, as the account of some event today. Yet it is correspondingly confused, and the difficulty is not to find facts but to find where they are leading. It is hard to take a long view of something that did not happen long ago and is indeed still going on. For the events about to unroll are the beginnings of the unfinished drama of European nationalism. On the chessboard of Europe, Vence—once no mean city and able to give a good account of itself in the factional wars of the olden past—is now but a pawn. If she has not shrunk actually, she has been so far surpassed as to be all but helpless in case of attack in force. Once she could even decide what side she would be on— king's party or Leaguers', Catholic or Protestant, Guelph or Ghibelline, pope or anti-pope. Henceforth she is never to be asked; she finds herself committed in advance, and situated on a permanent earthquake fault in European politics, a frontier where congested central Europe abuts uneasily against western Europe.

I go to the open windows and look out on this smiling land, little changed in centuries. There comes the sound of the church bells of Tourrettes, blowing softly around the shoulder of St. Raphaël Mountain, reminding me of sixteen centuries of Christianity in this spot. I can hear two men down on the road, calling to each other in patois. The soft, winy speech comes gurgling from their throats, and in so far as they speak their mother-tongue these folk are still Provençals, and Vençois, before they are Frenchmen.

Yet to be a Vençois today is not to be primarily a Provençal, or a Catholic, or to owe one's allegiance to some feudal overlord. The Vençois of today is officially and in his fate primarily a Frenchman, and France could, or her enemies could, force him to fight fellow-Catholics or even people close kin to the Provençals, the Catalans of Spain or the Piedmontese of Italy. For, from the eighteenth century onward, most European wars, however local in cause or initial extent, tend to become epidemic and engulf one country after another. The web of Europe cannot be torn anywhere without straining it to its farthest threads.

When I go into town I am reminded of how Vence is hostage to world history, by my friend the cobbler. He is a very big man—not fat but quite a giant in frame—who squeezes himself into a small shop, a hole in the wall of the Place Peyra. He has a heavy limp and some terrible scars in face and skull; science has patched him almost as thoroughly as it first messed him up. A German helmet, some vicious fragments of exploded steel, and a bayonet on his wall are all he has visibly to show for his pains. An unbroken sort of man, grim and almost violent, he won't make conversation with me, not even about the war souvenirs—regarding me quite properly as a foreigner, and a soft one at that, who was not present at the Chemin des Dames when he got his trophies and his wounds. He is, in short, a veteran, and there are millions like him all over Europe. When they went into the war in 1914, they were boys, like those in the streets of Vence now—strong, bronzed, full of zest, fond of plaguing the *gendarmes*, none too chaste, perhaps, or temperate, but planning ultimately a settled and laborious life full of duty and the rearing of children.

They planned, but fate was spun for them by three who sat in Vienna, Berlin, and St. Petersburg, respectively. The hatreds brewed in the cellars of Sarajevo sent my friend the cobbler to war. Now he is a man too big for the little shop and world that is left him, and he will never be able to do anything about it.

So, too, the little town had its plans, in the end of the seventeenth century. Vence, secure from wars during the time of Godeau and his immediate successors in the episcopal palace, enjoyed an era of prosperity, and climbed out of debt. In addition to its ramparts, town hall, public squares, the town now had its own mills, and was no longer forced to bring corn and olives to be ground at the mills of the seigneurs. It had its own looms, seven or eight tanneries, a pottery works, markets, and fairs. The cathedral was provided with a new organ, the old one being out of repair, too small, and "*indécente*" for a cathedral. There were a house of charity and a hospital, a school for choir boys, and the seminary which Godeau had founded. Louis XIV in 1693 bestowed upon the town the right to an escutcheon or armorial design. It showed, upon a shield, a little tower, for all the world like a castle on a chessboard, and over the shield arched crenelations, while round it ran a ribband bearing the proud words *Turris Civitatis Vencii.* Flanking the shield were two cornucopias spilling out the flowers and fruits that make Vence famous. By edict dated at Fontainebleau, October, 1699, the king conferred upon the town an establishment of police, symbol and proof that law and order no longer resided solely in the seigneurs but in the hands of the people too. Vence, cries old Tisserand, was now "at the height of her glory."

But all heights have crests, and downward slopes beyond them. And the War of the Spanish Succession was at hand in 1701. Louis XIV had just placed his grandson Philip on the throne of Spain. This united two powers that had formerly played off against each other, and thus the balance of power—already so called—was upset. Under the leadership of the Grand Monarch, France was preparing to push outward as far as it found weakness in Germany, the Low Countries, and Italy. Against her, united by mutual alarm, she had Austria, Portugal, Holland, Denmark, England, and part of Germany. And that Alp-straddling duchy of Savoy, which included Piedmont in Italy and the County of Nice.

Thus it came about that Spanish subjects of the Netherlands fought free Netherlanders. Bavarian Germans fought Austrian Germans. Frenchmen of the Dauphiné Alps did battle against Frenchmen of the Savoy Alps. And Vence, not ten miles from the Var River which separated France from Savoy, sent its young men to confront their relatives the Niçois.

Now Vence saw a continuous defile of French regiments marching through her territory, to defend the Var frontier. All the countryside joined in, and even little Tourrettes mustered out thirty men, each with three rounds of shot. But in March, 1704, the Savoyards crossed the Var, surprised Gattières in the night, and gave it up to pillage. In swift turn Cagnes, Le Broc, Carros, and Coursegoules were abandoned to the Savoyards and overrun. The refugees came pouring into Vence, among them the Seigneur Blacas of Carros and his wife—he whose family name, Good King René had said, was a synonym for valor. (Blacas left behind his old mother, but brought his silver plate.)

The turn of St. Jeannet soon came, and the people fled to a cave. When the soldiers, tipsy with wine and enflamed with loot, toiled up the slopes of the *baou*, the stout folk in the cave rolled down rocks upon them, shouting "Long live the King!"

The next night the Savoyards were at our gates. Vence surrendered, hoping to escape destruction, but many houses were pillaged. Innocent merchants saw their oil casks knocked open, their wine sent in a red river down the gutters or trickling into Savoyard bellies.

When the French returned in force, Vence was delivered by troops from Grasse and Draguignan. In 1706 French regiments again passed continually under our walls. Caught in the rains of St. Michel (a euphonious Provençal way of saying they were stuck in the mud), the French troops found themselves unable to budge their cannon. They were without food and without money, and demanded both of Vence.

Near starvation itself, Vence refused. The soldiery began to pillage. Finally the troops moved on, the rains having let up, and tramped away to a victory in the Alps.

Still, Vence found time and strength for family quarrels. Monsieur Vallier, the cook of the Marquis François de Villeneuve, was at outs with Maître Roux, the cook of Bishop de Bourcheneu, because the latter always got first choice of fish. So Vallier concealed himself, at eight o'clock of a July morning in 1706, in a shed near the fishmonger's, along with some confederates armed with staves, stones, and swords. As soon as Monsieur Pereimond, the fish merchant, arrived, Maître Roux presented himself with his basket and was promptly set upon by the lurking foe. At his cries, the domestics of the bishop hastened to his aid. There was a sharp skirmish, and Roux fled into the cathedral, dripping gore while the prelate's *valet de chambre* almost died of his wounds. Both sides rushed to court, and the marquis lost his case. All of which I relate because from personal experience I am able to state there is no feud like the feud between two French chefs. Obviously such little *contretemps* were, as they remain, the real business of Vence.

But her fate is still spun for her in distant capitals where kings, too, dispute their kettles of fish. They still speak here of 1707 as *l'an de la poou*, "the year of fear," when the natives had to "put lamp oil on their salads"—the same being, in those days, the bitter oil of rape-seed. Vence and her neighbors poured out men, money, and supplies for France. But once more the French troops retreated from the Var, and the hill towns were abandoned to Savoy.

Vence sent notables to entreat for clemency. But a ransom of thirteen hundred louis d'or was wrung from her and she was forced to quarter a troop of Hungarian soldiery, who rough-handled the citizens, pillaged the shops, and molested the womenfolk.

Though there was victory, the capture of Lerida, in 1708, the bonfires of rejoicing in Vence were dreary. French troops, taking the billets of their late enemies, took on some of their habits. Terrific rains washed the soil from the terraces; the crops failed; the town was near starvation. Louis XIV heard of its predicament, sent wheat, and gave employment by repairing the embankments of the Var. He exempted Vence and her neighbors from taxation for one year.

In that same year the Marquis of Vence became embroiled in a duel with the Chevalier of Grimaldi-Cagnes, at Toulon. Both gentlemen pierced each other's hearts at the same instant, and thus symbolically perished.

The Villeneuve family in these days was beginning more and more to inhabit Aix, the capital of Provence, and worldly Avignon. This was in imitation of the fashion of the great nobles of France who dwelt at Versailles or Fontainebleau or Paris, drawing their revenues from their estates but returning only to safeguard their interests, economize on their expenditures, or wait for storms to blow over. It was considered rustic to live on one's estates. To be banished to them was to languish in the ennui of exile. In proportion as the absentee-landlordism of the Villeneuves became more habitual, their relations with the commune became more and more unsympathetic and strained.

If possible, the year 1709 was leaner than 1707. In February the olives and oranges were killed in a great freeze. A Swiss regiment, quartered on Vence, demanded one thousand livres on instant payment. Upon refusal these allies, sent to protect the town, gave it over to pillage. They remained three years. The countryside was full of *barbets* or guerrillas. Owners of private houses, fleeing the town to escape the quartering of troops, found themselves robbed in the country. Hundreds of homeless wandered in town and countryside, sleeping in caves or in the porches of chapels. They lived by theft and, separately plying their trade, reunited at night, lit fires, gnawed the bones of their day's findings, drank, and "lived in debauch."

To meet this deplorable situation, the town's moneys were diverted to giving men employment in breaking stone on the road. Women were given spinning and knitting to do, while the children were set to weeding, collecting the big cones of the black pine (which make such fine kindling for the hearth, and still are brought to my door by children), and picking strawberries in the woods in June.

In 1727 there was called to this poor and remote little diocese Bishop Jean-Baptiste Surian, born at St. Chamas in Provence. He was one of ten brothers and almost as many sisters and, like many deeply religious persons, he had been a shepherd. At fourteen Surian ran away to Marseille with thirty-five sous, with which he purchased a little shoeshine box and set up for business on the street corner. There are several stories of what happened next. According to one, a priest came by and stopped for a shine. Noticing the maladroitness of the child, he bent down to help him, and the lad turned up a face of such intelligence and spirituality that the priest recommended him to the Fathers of the Oratory at Martigues. At any rate, there he was educated. He had a marvelous preaching voice, majestic presence, and a diction at once easy and brilliant. When he came to the episcopal palace at Vence, he was fifty-seven years old. And he could, it is said, have aimed much higher after he had preached before Louis XV and the court and been elevated to the Académie Française.

But Surian, like so many bishops before him, fell in love with Vence and would not leave her. He wrote: "I am more diverted in Vence than anywhere." And again, "In Paris the days seemed full, but at home, at night, one saw how empty they had been. Better have nothing to do than be busied with nothings." "Of Vence," he said, "I make a Paris, of my countryside a Versailles. The first science is to know how to be happy. This is certainly not the abode of the graces, but if one offered me Paris, I would prefer my sweet Vence."

Those who live here, and do not merely sojourn briefly, come soon to feel a sense of being at the core of life, so that all other places seem cold and grayer, sadder and less wise. The smell of the *rose de mai*, the song of the nightingale, the silver domes of the olives, the laughing and singing of the peasants, the chestnuts and wine of La Gaude upon the table—better things than these the planet does not offer. But there come times, especially in summer, when the little world of Vence seems to shrink, and decay in the sun. An old stench rises from the cellars and gutters that mingles with the smell of flowers, and it was this, I suppose, that made Godeau once call the place a "perfumed sow." The brooks are dry; the petals are fallen from the broom, and in the hills are only sunstroke and fierce thistles. It is so long to wait for sundown that the brown owl in the great ash outside the castle window begins to hoot for it at five in the afternoon. But night when it comes brings no nightingale. The bird is silent, molting. Even the sheep are gone, driven to the alpine meadows by their flockmasters. Every friend seems gone, and the voices of the peasants are alien. All this little world is alien; time stands still. And one remembers longingly that in other places great things are astir. Minds meet and strike sparks. Books are written and read. Symphonies are played, and heard by ears that understand them.

Probably every foreigner in Vence has known this revulsion. Godeau spoke of it. Surian must have known it, Academician that he was. He turned then for intellectual company and found it in the person of the wife of the seigneur, Madeleine de Villeneuve, whose grandmother was the Countess of Grignan, wife of the Governor of Provence, and that cold and conventional person immortal in the history of literature as the daughter of Madame de Sévigné and the unappreciative recipient of that great lady's letters.

But the young Marquise of Vence was, like her great-grandmother, a fascinating correspondent. In 1730 she records a trip from Vence to Le Bar, in company with Surian. "If I could paint the state of the roads for you I would. But your humble servant was not made for using such bad words." She probably followed the old Roman road, passing the chapel of Bon Voyage, going up and over Tourrettes, and down into the Gorges du Loup. This road, so enchanting in its views, in its flowers and odors, is now but a donkey trail, and was probably no better then. It is an excellent reminder of the painful and dilapidated nature of communication lines in Provence from the time of the Romans until the coming of the automobile.

Arrived at the château of Le Bar, writes Madeleine, "we tumbled off our horses into the courtyard, and greeted our noble hosts; everyone made four profound courtesies. I entered the hall which was lighted but lugubriously by four candles, between which awaited the mother of M. le Comte de Bar, who had recently broken her leg. The tapestries round the walls were five centuries old. They took me to a room where the floor was deep strewn with roses and jasmine; it took the breath away. I then went to the great hearth and baked myself out. When they came to lead me away it took a quarter of an hour to reach my bedroom. Here I found myself at the foot of a great bed so high that I had to climb up on a chair to get into it. . . . ."

Like Veranus of old, Surian combatted heresy, this time the gloomy dispute on Jansenism. The author of this trouble was Cornelius Jansen or Jansenius, Bishop of Ypres, feared by his students for his choleric temper and disliked by his chapter for his authoritarian ways. Deeply troubled by the theology of the Protestants about him, he tried to reform the Church from within, invoking a predestination more Calvinist than Calvin. He also charged the Jesuits with laxity and worldliness, with playing politics and granting absolution much too easily. And before his death—on which occasion Godeau had preached a eulogy in the cathedral—he had the satisfaction of seeing his tenets spread all through France. They became the focal point of a tendency in opposition to the complete authority of Rome.

Against all this the Jesuits raised a hue and cry. They succeeded in having Jansenism denounced from the Vatican, and the Jansenists were ultimately driven from the Church or to recantation. It all sounds very remote to us, but in Nice the Jansenists and anti-Jansenists fell upon each other with cudgels and knives. In Vence most of the cathedral chapter was Jansenist; more than half of the country priests of the diocese were of the persuasion. The other day I experimentally asked my rotund friend the curé about Jansenism. He rolled his eyes, and pursed his lips and tutted with them, while his fat hands made inexpressible gestures. Surian, it seems, did the little world of Vence a mighty turn when by his persuasive sweetness he brought his congregation back to conformity. I confess that an American and essentially protestant mind cannot weigh these matters with much hope of justice.

But now the twenty years of truce between Pan-European wars were over. Again power politics are clashing. France and Spain supported Bavaria and Prussia against Austria, England, Holland, Saxony, and Sardinia, in the eight years' War of the Austrian Succession. So once again the fault-line of the Var River frontier between France and Sardinia heaves, and Vence and all her neighbor villages trembled with the shock.

Vence was edified in 1746 by the passage of endless troops marching to defend the frontier against the Sardinians. The quartering of these allies was scarcely distinguishable from an invasion. A Majorcan regiment stole even the altar cloths. The French gave way, and Sardinians and Austrians, with brutal Croat mercenaries, were soon at the gates of Vence under the command of the honest old veteran Novaty. The Baron of Vence was blockaded in Antibes and had to surrender. Like Veranus of old, Surian went out to meet the barbarian. "General," he addressed Novaty, "you have not come to make war upon citizens but upon soldiers. The Lord of Hosts will decide whether your master or mine will conquer, but humanity and the generosity of the prince you serve forbid you to maltreat unarmed civilians." Impressed by the prelate's saintly aspect, Novaty gave strict orders to his soldiers. "How long will it take us to reach Lyons?" snapped a young Austrian aide. Surian turned to him coolly. "I know how long it would take me," he answered, "but I cannot say how long it will take you when you have to fight the troops of the King, my master."

Vence saw with well-grounded dread the approach of more foes, and this time she had to deal with General Maximilian Ulysses Browne (for whose Irish name I cannot account) and his Austrian hussars who were quartered for twenty days in 1747. The Vençois had to supply much oil and wine, and sheets and blankets for the officers. (The chroniclers of the town admit they gave only moth-eaten blankets.) In the spirit of barbaric wantonness the Croats marched up to the château of Malvans, so linked with memories of the Templars and legends of Queen Jeanne, and set the torch to it.

Help at last came to stricken Vence when Marshal Belle-Isle drove out the Austrians and Sardinians. But the quartering of French troops proved appallingly costly. Again the debt of Vence soared into realms almost unpayable. When peace came in 1748, it was for Vence the peace of exhaustion. The quarreling kings had too long had their way with her, and with all the villages of all the many-colored lands on Europe's map. By their bloody and conscienceless disputes, they might gain a province here and aggrandize themselves there. They could not perceive that they were preparing their own downfall, squandering their heritage, and tearing apart the old regime, the last vestiges of feudal society.

CHRONOLOGY FOR CHAPTER NINE

KINGS OF FRANCE

1643 Louis XIV
1715 Louis XV

BISHOPS OF VENCE

1672 Louis Thomassin
1681 Théodore Allart
1686 Jean de Viens
1697 François de Berton de Crillon
1701 Flodoard Moret de Bourcheneu
1727 Jean-Baptiste Surian
1754 Jacques de Grasse
1758 François Gabrielle Moreau

SEIGNEURS OF VENCE

1657	Claude II (nephew of Gaspard)	m. Catherine de Grasse
1667	Alexandre (son), first Marquis of Vence	m. Marie-Marguerite de Brancas
1699	François-Sextius (son)	m. Jeanne Millot
1706	Alexandre-Gaspard (son)	m. Madeleine-Sophie de Simiane

permission; the revelers are beginning the drum; a priest accompanied a bridal time to the baron only. The young man with his raised or lost excited that permission. They shout to the musicians to begin

Chapter Ten

REVOLUTION AND EMPIRE

THE SCENE IS THE PUBLIC SQUARE OF VENCE. THE YEAR is 1762. And the young folk are dancing a farandole. It is early spring; the square is lively with flower vendors; gillyflowers, pink, purple, and white, and anemones, scarlet and purple, violets, and hyacinths splash color against the gray of the old stone walls. The waters of the fountain flash and laugh; the bells of the cathedral toll a merry clangor. Young bucks are buying flowers for the black hair of their sweethearts-of-an-hour, and little nosegays to tuck in the bodices drawn so tight over the round breasts. A continual stream files in and out of the wineshops. The fun is getting tipsy. And more than wine is mounting to the heads of the dancers, whirling around to the ancient tunes, merry and childish as nursery songs, that are tootled on the Provençal flutes, and accented with the long, Moorish, dogskin drums. Youth's rebellion is in the air. There is a buxom impudence in the flying skirts of the girls, and a rowdy animalism in the laughter of the young men. Suddenly the whirling ceases; the drums are still. A man-at-arms, sent down from the château, orders the musicians to cease and in the name of the seigneur demands to know by whose permission the revelers are beating the drum, a privilege accorded since feudal times to the baron only.

The youngsters say that the mayor has granted that permission. They shout to the musicians to begin again; someone proposes dancing under the marquis' window. The idea is joyfully taken up, and reeling and singing, shouting and kissing, they flaunt their farandole under the window of the outraged nobleman, who bangs shut the casement and sits down to write out a complaint to the Intendant of Grasse.

The following May, on St. Lambert's Day, the fun was noisier than before. This time the permission of the police was alleged by the merrymakers.

But there were more serious bones of contention among the burgesses, the bishop, and the baron, and it is significant that, as the Revolution is preparing, the old animosity between bishop and baron has

170

broken down. Proud were the two co-seigneurs of Vence, the unyielding and dominant Bishop Moreau and Seigneur Jean Alexandre Romée de Villeneuve, Field Marshal, whose marriage contract to a La Rochefoucauld had been signed by Louis XV and his queen, the Dauphin, and Marie-Josephine of Saxony. And they drew together, these two representatives of institutions with vested interests, into an alliance against the growing power of the people.

Perhaps they realized now, the nobles and the prelates, that to maintain their power they ought all along to have presented a solid front against the franchise of the town. They must have guessed that their age-long rivalry had been a tactical mistake which had permitted the pretentions of the people to take shape. They must have felt the prescience of change, and change is dangerous to traditional privileges and wealth. But it was too late; the people had found voice to ask questions, and the claims of feudalism and the articles of religion are sustained only by grace of faith.

One of the pertinent questions was this: Who should command the ramparts of Vence? The marquis said, "I, for I am the chief man-at-arms of the commune, the natural leader, the only person with a tradition of military training and instinct." The bishop said, "I, for I am the warden of the holy house of God round which the ramparts are but a shell." The people

171

said, "We, for our forefathers built the walls with the sweat of their backs; it is we who man them; the counts of Provence and the kings of France have granted us the right to keep the city keys, and we have never been behindhand in the paying of royal tithes."

The fief of the commune of the Malvans was another sore point. It had been bought outright by the town of Vence, the consuls were thus its seigneurs, and every Vençois had some rights in it. Unfortunately the title was not unencumbered. The Seigneur of Vence still retained here his ancient hunting rights. And one morning as a citizen, gun across his shoulder, stepped onto the fief of the Malvans, the marquis' gamekeeper ordered him to give up his gun. The man refused. The gamekeeper fired; the man turned and ran and was chased down the road toward Vence by the gamekeeper (now off the fief) and was shot and nearly killed. Town and marquis rushed to court.

"The inhabitants of Vence," said the Intendant scornfully, "have long been insolent, rebellious, ungrateful and insubordinate." The advocates of the seigneurie cried to the courtroom, "This little town, lost in the mountains, gives itself the airs of grandeur and independence. A seigneurial fief wants to exist like an independent republic. It would pass as the equal of Grasse, of Marseille, of Aix! It names its consuls, who think themselves the equals of the seigneur!"

Vence could and did reply that they were indeed a city. That they had been granted by the kings of France the rights of taxation, of control of public expenses, of fixing the tariffs on public utilities, of guarding the walls, of keeping police, of holding the offices of mayor, controller, etc. That they had always paid every sou of tribute to the Crown. That in the city were masters of all trades. They had a cathedral, an *hôtel de ville*, a public square, and ramparts that had withstood great sieges. Surely Vence had earned a city's dignity.

It was noticed when the judge entered the courtroom that he bowed deeply to all the nobles. The result of the trial was probably predestined in the best Jansenist style. The town lost its case in the dispute over the commune of the Malvans, and besides paying an amende of six thousand pounds and costs, the consuls of Vence were compelled to beg pardon of the seigneur on bended knee. The town took its defeat with a singularly cheerful spirit, and the consuls lost none of their swagger. Perhaps it was a slight balm to their wounded pride that the court allowed them the right to order the drums to be beaten.

But this setback in the progress of municipal liberty was immaterial, for the sands of time, both for the nobility and for the clergy, are running out. Pisani, last Bishop of Vence, of a noble family of La Gaude, in his relations with the town was as intransigent in tem-

173

poral matters as he was personally clement; but the crozier too will glitter only a little longer in the gray and twisted streets of the town. Dangerous streets that will ring soon to the trampling of angry mobs washing like a flood from wall to wall.

But the kindly Pisani suspects nothing; he dreams of the glorious line of the bishops of Vence; absently he pats the heads of the beautiful dirty children. Withdrawing from worldly cares, he goes alone to St. Martin, there to picnic in the shade of the Templars' house, to meditate upon the blue heaven of God, and to listen to the missel thrush and blackbird.

So, while the forces of the Revolution were actually gathering, the life of Vence went on, in that fascinating way of historical moments, when humanity is like a crowd of passengers on a boat, eating, drinking, loving, and fighting, while all the time, unknown even to the helmsman, the ship is borne swifter and swifter toward a cataract. The course of events seemed sleepily to flow on unchanged. True, times were hard. In 1788 a bank failure in Marseille brought a repercussion of misery in Vence. A series of severely cold winters brought disastrous results upon a population subsisting entirely by agriculture and above all by flowers and fruits. In Vence the *hôtel de ville* was in a ruined condition; public mills and ovens were also dilapidated; land values were poor, cash money scarce. Even the people knew that the finances of the

174

court were fantastic. The peasant hid his sou in his stocking; the townsman lay awake o' nights and worried for the future.

Now and then a lively happening relieved the sleepy depression of the countryside. One such was the capture of Gaspard de Besse, the Robin Hood of Provence, who haunted the Estérel Mountains and the Auberge des Adrets (which still stands) and had, too, a hidy-hole in a cave near St. Jeannet. The people idolized him, and when in 1776 he was broken on the wheel at Aix it made a greater stir in Vence than the obscure fact that about that time the English colonists in America decided to defy their king.

But before that distant war was done Admiral de Grasse, brother to a Bishop of Vence, was to blockade the English with his fleet at Yorktown; the King of France was to lend to the American Revolutionists money sorely needed at home, to spite the English; and some strange shibboleths were to waft back across the ocean. It appeared that all men were born equal; that man had some natural rights. That kings and governments were not invincible.

So far as Vence is concerned, the Revolution began when the King convoked at Versailles the Estates-General, and earlier the provincial assemblies. So the Estates of Provence—suppressed for the last one hundred and forty-seven years—met again at Aix, on the last day of the year 1788. Bishop Pisani of Vence was there, the Bishop of Grasse too, all the nobility and the deputies of the clergy and communes. Vence, having failed to elect her mayor as a delegate, saw herself represented by Jean-Joseph Mougins de Roquefort, Mayor of Grasse. Soon he was writing excitedly to Vence, from the stormy deliberations of the Assembly, that a new era of liberty was dawning.

Now—so the Vençois learned from the letters of Mougins—the Assembly had proclaimed sweeping changes. The property of church and lord was to become taxable, like that of commoners. All seigneurial courts were abolished; henceforth justice was to be administered by state and communal authority. Purchase of offices was abrogated; appointments would be made on the basis of merit. Any citizen might now ply any trade, or enter civil or military service. Ended were many an ancient task and tithe once laid by the seigneur on the shoulders of his people.

Obligingly, the Marquis of Vence wrote from Aix to the Mayor of Vence that for his part he was ready to waive all revenues from his fief and to sustain his part in taxation toward public works. Though he was thereupon praised throughout Provence as one of the most enlightened of the nobility, no sooner was the yoke lifted from the people of Vence than they discovered, to their indignation, how heavy it had been, and how sore it had rubbed them. Instead of gratitude, they felt a contagion of hatred, directed not toward the heavy-handed, haughty seigneurs of the past, but against the present marquis who had yielded so much, the excellent Pierre-Paul-Ours-Hélion de Villeneuve. So high did feeling run in the town that the marquis, from Paris, directed his family to remove to the residence of the Governor of Provence. And even here they were followed by the howls and threats of the populace. Again the marquis dipped quill in ink and sorrowfully wrote to the mayor: "It is painful for me that in the unhappy circumstances in which we find ourselves today, I have not the hope of considering as a refuge a spot so long and constantly inhabited by our fathers. . . . . I think, however, that the greater part of you still wish me well, and it is this persuasion that causes me to write to you and that encourages me to place under your safeguard my wife, my children, indeed all that I hold most precious."

The municipal council replied with distressed assurances of esteem, and deprecation of the behavior of a few lawless persons, and so forth and so forth. The letters are courteous enough on both sides, and, as they drift apart, the people and the seigneur seem still to be reaching across a void, not wide as yet, to shake hands with just a little too much good will. Actually, neither side has any control over the currents that are bearing them apart.

Reason as well as wrath strengthened these currents. For the nobility, once it began to measure its privileges in terms of logic and of democratic justice, discovered that there was no more reason why one feudal privilege should stand than another. To be consistent (and logical thought was the god of the aristocrats, or they believed it was), the *ancien régime* would have had to abolish itself, and that is just what, in the first or constitutional phase of the Revolution, it was doing. For each noble, of course, there was some point at which he decided that things had gone far enough and too far. At that point he would resist, indignantly, and at that point the illusion of good will between seigneur and people would be shattered; the strained handclasp across the widening gulf would break.

For the Marquis of Vence, the breaking-point came when, not long after his return to Vence in April of 1790, the commune demanded from him his private pews in the cathedral. The marquis objected; Vence wrote excitedly to the National Assembly that to allow De Villeneuve to keep his pews would be, in effect, to hold back the dawn of the new day. A church pew seems a sorry thing to stumble over, but on it our little local Revolution finally broke. Pierre-Paul-Ours-Hélion de Villeneuve—no doubt a mild and reasonable man—was obliged, like all the nobles of his age, to meet the monstrous debt compounded by his forebears through the past.

How it was that he escaped his angry fellow-citizens the good Tisserand does not tell, but another abbé, the present incumbent, related it to me as he had heard it, while we stood together under the castle wall with the sound of the fountain in our ears. The Seigneur of Vence, so I was told, had his servants hide him in an empty wine barrel which, among full casks, was put on a cart and trundled down to Cagnes, whence De Villeneuve made his way to Nice. His relative, Joseph-César de Villeneuve, Seigneur of Tourrettes, took his son and fled on foot down the steep rocks below the town, into the valley of the Loup, and so through the woods to Cagnes and on to Nice. Once in Nice, over the Var frontier, they and many another fleeing noble found themselves in the safety of the Kingdom of Sardinia. Here they could compare their trials, await the arrival of relatives and servants who might have smuggled out jewels and money, and plot how to regain their lost domains. As the number of these *émigrés* grew, the threat of them became evident, and the arrests of those in flight came fast, many taken hereabout being sent to prison in Grasse.

Everywhere National Guards were forming—popular armies, as contrasted with the old royal troops; everywhere there was a sense of impending danger, no one knew from just what source. Sardinia was about to attack; the emigrant nobles were about to stage a counterrevolution; Austria, Prussia, England—

all were in league against the liberty of the French. Like most revolutionaries, these were hypersuspicious; they saw something sinister in every event, and when half a hundred hungry vagrants roamed the *baous* above Vence, the tale grew into a mighty host of brigands that caused messengers to fly from Vence to Tourrettes, from Tourrettes to Castellane, from there to Coursegoules. Each town had National Guards in it, and each constantly clamored for more protection.

On December 22, 1790, the guards garrisoning the Lérins Islands effected the release of the prisoners incarcerated in the sun-scorched old fortress where, a century before, the Man in the Iron Mask had passed so many weary years. Seven prisoners emerged, some of whom had rotted there for thirty years. Only the Comte de Monteil, who had been there longest, refused to leave, declaring the spot should be his tomb. The others, and the soldiers, did a farandole together. So on our stage, too, there is a little Bastille. As soon as it was empty of victims of the royal displeasure, it began to receive those of popular displeasure.

The spirit of class warfare and of anticlericalism, reaching through the provinces by the spring of 1790, was slow in coming to Provence, the most remote and easygoing of all the counties of France. The Bastille had fallen nine months before, when at last mob violence really got under way in Provence. At first this was in the western part of the province only, and so

Vence, still itself at peace, saw the arrival, in full flight, of the bishops of Noyon and Toulouse, who refuged at the episcopal palace with Bishop Pisani. But when they went to the house of Blacas, the notary, a mob gathered outside the windows, threatening death to the bishops. The authorities came, and the crowd, muttering, was dispersed. But Pisani himself heard further warning. Walking in the fields, he encountered the town surgeon—a lowly caste of individual in those days—out hunting. "We shall soon be using these"—he promised insolently, patting his fowling piece—"on some of you bigger game." Times are changing, Seigneur Pisani de la Gaude, Monseigneur de Vence. Do you understand, godly autocrat? Do you hear the trampling *sabots* of Time?

For a while it had seemed that Church and people would keep in step. As the troops of Vence marched off to the Var frontier to meet the menace of Sardinia and the *émigrés*, Bishop Pisani had blessed the flags. The town voted 1,026 livres toward the national defense, and patriotism resounded from sea to mountains. But the Assembly did not spare the Church. It enjoined upon all ecclesiastics an oath of allegiance which put the nation above all else, even allegiance to Rome. Those who took the oath—and many did so, especially among the humbler clergy—were accounted "constitutional" priests, recognized by the state and authorized to perform marriages, register baptisms, and the like. The nonjurors, or those priests who refused to take the oath, were left, legally, without rights and even subject to charges of treason.

Of the nonjuring clergy, Bishop Pisani himself was the leader. When ordered to vacate the episcopal palace, in accordance with a national decree that sequestered all Church property, he yielded at once, silence his only protest. On his escutcheon over the wall he wrote, before he left, the long farewell of the bishops of Vence: "Aequus dominus dedit, Dominus abstulit. Sit nomen Domini benedictum." Then he locked the doors, delivered the keys to the mayor, and took up residence in a citizen's home. But having rendered unto Caesar what was Caesar's, this soldier of the cross surrendered nothing that was God's. Next Sunday he was in the cathedral to say Mass as usual, and from the pulpit he announced his intention of remaining, although his once most trusted curé, having taken the oath, struggled to usurp his place. The chapter of the cathedral was split in twain. Over the tumult rose the voice of Pisani. "If I had my jurisdiction from the hands of men, I would cede it as a proof of my fidelity to the nation and the law of the King; but I received it entirely from Jesus Christ and from his Vicar on earth. . . . . I should exercise that jurisdiction even were the state to proscribe the Catholic religion."

Threatened with prison, Pisani on May 21, 1791,

fled at last to Nice, and most of the nonjuring clergy were sooner or later constrained to follow him. From across the Sardinian frontier, Pisani hurled at Vence the pope's pastoral letter, denouncing the constitutional priests and declaring all their offices null and void. Friendly hands fixed it, on the night of June 12, to the cathedral door.

On that very day the commune of Vence bought in from the government the bishop's palace, for fourteen thousand livres of paper money. But the effect of the pastoral letter was immediate. The curé Vial said Mass to an empty cathedral. All through the diocese the constitutional clergy found itself neglected, particularly by women—always the bulwark of a faith. The Roman, or nonjuring, clergy stole back across the border by night to perform marriages and baptisms and all those sacraments that touch the very springs of woman's life.

While France was internally torn with suspected and actual revolution and counterrevolution and with strife within the Church, the menace of foreign intervention, at first only a dark suspicion, was becoming a reality. The reactionary monarchies of Prussia and Austria had formed an alliance against her. The Kingdom of Sardinia (nucleus of the future Kingdom of Italy under the House of Savoy) took serious alarm at the state of affairs just across her frontier of the Var. From beyond the Channel, Britain could see the whole structure of society, based as it was then thought to be upon royalty, nobility, religion, and property, trembling and falling. France, the richest and most cultivated nation in the world, was turning to anarchy. It was as if the keystone of the European arch should crumble, and all her neighbors were now preparing for intervention if necessary.

Revolutionary France was well aware of the ring of foes around her. Vence, like every least town, prepared for war. She sent all but one of her bells to be melted up for cannon. One of the first to go was the new one, given but a few years before by the Marquise of Vence herself. Gold, silver, and jewels were stripped from the cathedral, to be sold for the good of the nation. The silver busts of St. Veranus and St. Lambert, which pious generations believed had saved the town from plague and siege, were rammed into a sack with kicks of the boot and sent away to be sold and melted up.

Now on the march to the Sardinian frontier, French troops began to pour into the countryside, demanding food, demanding money, and ridiculing the raw and rustic volunteer companies of Vence. The old town suffered another of those invasions by her countrymen, and she responded sulkily. Hardheaded peasants looked askance at promissory notes and requisitions signed by outland generals. Further, nobody really liked the French and Flemish troops. It must be re-

membered that Provençal people did not then con-
sider themselves wholly French, except politically.
The Midi people thought of the northern French with
the suspicion and distaste with which the inhabitants
of Louisiana might have viewed a Massachusetts regiment quartered on them. The troops made reprisals,
by seizing what they needed. Someone's cabbage
patch was invaded by the soldiery. Neighbors fired
in defense of the cabbages. The troopers fired back.
General Somebody upbraided Vence for want of patriotism. Vence felt that patriotism began at home and
pillaging abroad.

Vence herself was in an ecstacy of patriotism.
"Arms, give us arms!" cried the Vençois, writing to
the Assembly. "If the enemy dares to set foot on the
sacred soil of liberty, we will teach him what the patriotism of eight hundred National Guards of Vence
can be!"

Up and down in the square outside the Peyra gate,
that had once been the garden of Godeau, a brainy
little officer named Masséna was drilling the troops,
men of Ardennes and Flanders, raw country boys of
Grasse and Vence, whipping them into shape to fight
the Revolution's enemies. Masséna was one of those
dashing, showy Napoleonic butchers who still have
the power, like the sound of a drum, to stir the heart
against the judgment of the head. Soon he was to win
his first dazzling successes, and Napoleon would call

him "Victory's darling child." Son of a tradesman, born near Nice, Masséna's rocket rose till it excited the envy of the Corsican. Plenty of excuses for bringing him down could be found when needed. Undependable, dishonest, insubordinate, cruel, he represented all that was worst in the Mediterranean character, yet Nice has named its finest square in his honor, and weekly in the honking, swirling pageant of the Place Masséna, I stop to sip a *fine*, while waiting for the bus to take me back to that quiet hill town that he left when his battalion marched away on the eighteenth of June, 1792.

Strange and terrible *annus Domini* Ninety-three, when the Christian year was abandoned, and it became the Year One of the Republic! The old provinces of France had been done away with, and names rich in nine centuries of association were obliterated—Provence, Normandy, Burgundy, Lorraine, Aquitaine—to give place to arbitrary and mechanical *départements*, deliberately cut at right angles to old provincial lines in order to break up the spirit of separatism and to create national unity. Vence found herself in the *département* of Var, and in the *viguerie* of St. Paul. The neighboring town of St. Paul, long despised as an insignificant rival, was made chief town of the *viguerie*. And Vence was left without even her bishopric, her cathedral. From this hour dates the downfall of her one-time importance, her reduction in stature from that of a city to that of a small town. All this was something on which the proud inhabitants had never calculated; they petitioned, and they stormed, but all to no avail. They fought the St. Paulois with fists and knives, and the St. Paulois fought back. The ancient enmity between Grasse and Antibes flared up in a similar warfare. All over the land there was anarchy between village and village. Something like the chaos of the Dark Ages was returning.

On September 20, 1792, the French defeated the Prussians at the Battle of Valmy, and the next day the Convention in Paris declared royalty at an end. So the First Republic came into being, and on the twenty-eighth the troops at Vence took the oath of undying hatred for royalty, and of loyalty to the Convention.

Now at last the emboldened French, having driven back the Prussians, decided to end for once and all the threat of Sardinia across the Var, and of the émigrés gathered at Nice. The troops so long quartered at Vence and Antibes, Grasse and Cagnes, were hurled across the Var in September of 1793. In Nice the wildest confusion reigned. A crowd of panic-stricken fugitives jammed the road over the Maritime Alps to Turin. Priests, monks, nuns, Sardinian troops, noble émigrés and their families and servants, civilian officials, and common men, women, and children, formed a long train winding up to the historic pass, the Col di Tenda. Every sound of hoofbeats in the rear was thought to be the pursuing cavalry of Masséna, so fugitives fired on more fugitives behind. The sufferings of the Marquise de Villeneuve and her children in the rains of St. Michel especially aroused the compassion of all who beheld them.

When Nice was captured, those who remained went mad with Revolutionary fervor. In the confusion, Canon Mars, one of the bravest of the nonjuring clergy of Vence, slipped back into the old diocese, there to be captured by two dragoons, carried in chains to Grasse, and executed the next year. Pisani, too, was captured, brought to Aix for trial, defended himself—he had once studied for the law—with dignity and even humor, and was acquitted.

In Grasse the Terror was in full swing. A guillotine was set up in the once happy little city, and so was a temple to the "Religion of Reason." In Vence the cathedral was sacked a second time to glean the last vessels of gold and silver. The last bell was dismounted and melted up. No Masses were said in any church or wayside chapel, even by the constitutional clergy, which had been excommunicated from Rome. Only in the caves of St. Jeannet, a few brave priests did homage to the Virgin, a few frightened peasants came by stealth to hear them.

For centuries, in Vence, had stood a Way of Calvary, a circuit on the stony hills southwest of town, through the oak woods of La Conque, where the feet of the devout had long been wont to tread the round of fourteen chapels, or stations, of the Cross, representing the passion of Christ. By no means uncommon in Brittany and Spain, such circuits are rare in Provence. The wooden carvings, depicting the way of Christ from the Annunciation to the Crucifixion, were the work of some naïve but fervent artist whose name is now forgotten. But they were the Passion Play, made living in wood, of this ancient Christian town.

On December 20, 1793, the chapels were destroyed, and the carvings and holy relics were brought to the public square before the *hôtel de ville* and piled up in a huge bonfire. "Let us see," cried Mayor Maurel of Vence, "how well this wood of Calvary will warm us," and so saying he set a burning crucifix to the pyre. The pious would have us believe that the smoke suffocated him, and he fled choking toward the *hôtel de ville;* at its doors a stroke of apoplexy felled him to the ground. But no miracle spared the ancient carvings as their flames leaped to the sky.

From this event the Vençois received the nickname of *les brûle-bon-Dieu,* or "God-burners." Vigorously the Vençois deny it; a patriotic historian has claimed that this was the deed of the Huguenot troops in the Ardennes regiment stationed in Vence. You may think as you prefer about this; I fear that Vence took the contagion of antireligions fever, along with the rest of Revolutionary France.

In Paris, the Terror was going from madness to madness; the Revolution, like Saturn, was devouring its children. The Hebertists were guillotined in March of 1794, the Dantonists in April, the Robespierrists in July. Then came the great reaction. Suddenly everyone was sick of violence and accusations and bloodshed. Vanoly, the worst of the Terrorists in Vence, was sent to the penal colony of Cayenne. All the Robespierrists were thrown into prison. Among its victims was a Corsican officer, suspected of leanings toward Robespierre, who was jailed in Antibes. Soon released, he walked from Nice to Vence, and wandered through our streets without being recognized by anyone as the future emperor of the French, Napoleon Bonaparte.

Still, republican sentiment ran high. Vence planted a Tree of Liberty; she was delirious with processions and republican hymns. In 1796 this Bonaparte fellow, so the Vençois learned, was preparing to march into Italy, and carry fear to Austria.

Behind him, the Provençal land existed in an uneasy state bordering on anarchy. The mountains were full of guerrillas. Nobody knew where the government stood, or what the laws were. Resort to arms was the final answer to every dispute. From 1796, when Napoleon invaded Italy, to his return from Egypt, all was turmoil in Vence. It was easy to make resounding speeches, to march about and shout, *"Ça ira, ça ira, et ça tiendra! Vive la République!"* It was harder to restore order, to settle down to work. Vence let its Sacred Flame of the Republic go out, and received a reprimanding letter from the Directory. But now came the *coup d'état* of the 18 *Brumaire*, by which Napoleon Bonaparte became Consul of France—first step upon the road to empire. In 1804 that Empire was proclaimed, and Vence lit joyful bonfires. In the churches, the altars were raised again.

Napoleon had made Pisani, so Vence heard, Bishop of Namur. It heard, too, of the only son of its old seigneur. Young Clément-Louis-Hélion was off to the wars. Thrice in one summer he was wounded in Germany; all through the terrible Russian campaign of 1812, he fought. And I suppose that many a humbler son of Vence was at Austerlitz and Wagram, Jena or Eylau, Lützen or Dresden.

But the history of Vence itself is lost to me from the beginning of the Empire to the return from Elba, when Bonaparte sat to rest on the shore at Golfe Juan and a butcher of Cannes shot at and narrowly missed the butcher of Europe. The clash of the fountain of Vence, the laughter of its sheep bells on the hills, are drowned in the noise of the drums and the guns.

With the restoration of the Bourbons in 1815, "that *émigré*, de Villeneuve," whose estates had become forfeit in the Revolution, was once again Seigneur of Vence, Marquis of Greolières and Garde-Adhemare, Lord of St. Laurent-la-Bastide, Puget-Treize-Dames, and St. Étienne-des-Ports. That same year he died and was succeeded by his son Clément-Louis-Hélion, the Napoleonic veteran, who dwelt in Paris, a member of the House of Peers.

On December 16, 1819, the lord of Vence wrote to its mayor, feeling out the way for his return, though as no more than a visitor who wished to view again "the old château of my youth." All bygones were to be forgotten, he assured the town, and no one, he expressly stated, was to plan a reception for him. "I ask of you only the smallest chamber with two mattresses on the floor, one for me and one for the Count of Thorenc, my friend, who is travelling with me."

So, three days before Christmas, the last Seigneur of Vence returned to the roof of his fathers. What personal memories of tender family life he had, we cannot know, though they must have crowded thick about him. Life in the old regime of France had courtesies and beauties, so De Tocqueville has told the world, which were perpetuated only by tradition; once lost, they vanished without trace and could not even be imagined save by the last survivors who remembered them. The Marquis of Vence must have recalled them, lying on his mattress, in remote, bright, happy pictures of a lucky childhood, and then, at the violent turn of fortune's wheel, in those scenes of the Terror—the angry crowds, the threats of death, his own flight with his mother and sisters.

Now the madness of the Revolution was over, and ended too were the feudalism and the abuses that had brought it on. France had at last become the seat of liberty, equality, and fraternity, where a nobleman, asking no privilege of his humblest fellow-citizens, could without fear come home among them. He could stand safely in the cold, deserted halls of his ancestors and feel running warm and proud within him the blood of all those noble men and women who had colored and troubled the countryside for centuries, the males with names as proud as stags: Scipion and César, Roumiou and Hugues; and of all those noble dames, their bedfellows, with names as sleek as does: Douce and Dulceline, Alasacie and Aicarde, Françoise, Cécile, and Angélique.

In 1834 the Marquis of Vence, peer of France, field marshal, and grand commander of the Legion of Honor, died in Paris, last male of the direct line.

So it is over, the grandeur and the privilege and the presumption. The one-time cathedral is now merely a provincial church. The barons, like the bishops, have departed, never to return. In place of the episcopate is the simple priesthood of today, embodied in the curé, who in all weathers, his black skirts flapping and his shovel hat tilted against the wind, trundles

193

about the parish serving his everlasting flock. For the people of Vence are the only survivors of the ancient order. Still today are heard such noble names as Blacas and Bérenger, Roubaud and Guigou; they are borne now by tradesmen and artisans, and borne, I may say, with more honor and credit than by some of those old mountain barons who from their castle keeps robbed and oppressed their fellow-men, rode their hunters through his grain, and humbled his daughters. It is by virtue of a perdurable average rightness that the common people have at last emerged triumphant. Theirs is the heritage of the centuries; to them belongs the town that was, by the unwritten freehold of hearthfire and rooftree, always their own. Once, in the Middle Ages, it called itself a city, a cathedral city. It is little more than a village today, a gray old wrinkled town, but alive, indomitably alive, and ripening even now the seeds of tomorrow.

CHRONOLOGY FOR CHAPTER TEN

KINGS OF FRANCE
House of Bourbon

1774   Louis XVI

THE FIRST REPUBLIC

1792   The Convention
1795   The Directory
1799   The Consulate

THE FIRST EMPIRE

1804   Napoleon I

House of Bourbon (restored)

1814 Louis XVIII
1824 Charles X
1830 Louis-Philippe

BISHOPS OF VENCE

1763 Michel-François Couet de Vivier de Lorry
1769 Jean Cairol de Medaillon
1771 Antoine-René de Bardonneche
1783 Charles Pisani de la Gaude

SEIGNEURS OF VENCE

1770	Jean-Alexandre Romée	*m.* Angélique-Louise de la Roche-foucauld
1786	Pierre-Paul-Ours Hélion	*m.* Marie-Clémentine de Laage
1815	Clément-Louis Hélion	*m.* Aymardine-Marie-Juliette d'Harcourt

(In 1834 the direct male line became extinct.)

195

Postscript

So HERE I LEFT VENCE, ENDING MY BRIEF ACCOUNT OF long event, and quitting, soon, the little town myself. It was in spring, I remember, that we drove away from it, my wife and our two laughing little boys. The countryside was laughing with them, for the almond trees were in blossom all up the great gray slopes, and so was the borage along the roadside, and the blue bugle. The road out of Vence winds down toward Nice, following the Lubiane's stony thin course, passing the doughty little silhouette of St. Paul across the shining valley. And all the way our friends the peasants made us farewell, here a gnarled oldster looking up from his digging to answer the children's wave, there a young woman waving too, from her doorway with the grapevine trained above it and the Bordeaux mixture spattered in soft blue on the old stone of the wall. So, mile by mile, we left it behind us, the town that had for three years been our town, our home town—left it, we thought, secure in its long and varicolored history, like the hero of an old fairy story who lives happily ever after.

I seldom heard, in the years that followed, from any of my friends there. The closest of them were not the writing kind; they felt, I think, as I certainly felt, that words were not needed between us. Between perfect friends silence is often a mark of companionability, and if they thought of me as happy in that fabulous land of America, I thought of them as blessed and secure in a way of life tested through centuries. So well did I know that way that, an ocean and a continent away, I could say when Madame Pons would be picking her tea roses for the Paris market, when Monsieur Roeder would be making his wine, purpling himself to the elbows, and when my good *femme de ménage* Thérèse would begin to worry again about shoes for her little boy to trot to school in.

Perhaps I could recall the seasons of Vence the more vividly because I gravitated, presently, to Santa Barbara—farther off from Provence than any other part of the United States, yet closest to it in scene and climate. Winter rains, and spring that comes in

197

winter, the sheen of olives blowing silver in the wind, the perfume of orange blossoms and of the foaming little yellow tree that here is not *mimosa* but acacia, and the rearing arid mountains softening so tenderly to blue at twilight—these, with the level sea line always making the southern horizon, must have determined why I came to live here. For they brought the same happiness I had known in Provence.

God knows I had been happy there. If France was not the country of my birth, my pride, and my allegiance, it was, in the words of a Frenchman, "the country of my heart." Two of my children were born there and one died there, and there, unwatched, uncriticized, I found my first uncertain voice as a writer. And France is so hospitable to lovers that for two to leave it is like shutting the door upon a bridal chamber.

When France fell, in June of 1940, thousands of Americans must have felt as I did—that something intimately their own had been dishonored and destroyed. Southeastern France, of course, was unoccupied then by the Germans. I had three letters, all told, from friends in Vence at that time, and they seemed hardly to speak of the Provence I knew. It was as if no sun shone there any more.

On November 11, 1942, in answer to the American and British landings in North Africa, the Germans and Italians seized upon Provence and all of unoccupied France. Now once more, as in the Dark Ages, there are no records for my little chronicle of Vence. For twenty-one dragging months there is silence, and sorrowing thoughts. Then comes a date for me to give you—the last date in this little history. It is August 29, 1944—the day on which American troops, under General Patch, entered Vence and set it free.

We did not come as liberators with only a noble disinterest in the town we succored. Ours was not the philanthropic heroism of the knight that slays the dragon so that a maiden may be unchained. We came —and our future, together with Vence's, depends upon our all understanding this—we came as neighbors, to help a village threatened only more acutely than the little towns of our own land.

It cost us blood. Resistance, I learn from the scant War Department communiqués I can procure, was fiercest at Cagnes. That is only six miles from Vence. Probably—I cannot here be historically definite, for at this writing communications have not yet been re-established between Provence's citizenry and our own —probably those boys from little American towns spent their young blood upon the ancient cobbles of Vence too. Certain it is they had the will to, if needs must. They who fought for America in the streets of an old French town knew well that the battle line stretches unbroken from the Peyra gate to their own front doors.

For free Americans sleep, and may be bound with chains as they slumber, while they delude themselves that they can ever be free of Europe's burden of the centuries. True that our land was new, our bold political idea was new, when first we founded this nation. But the American is not a new man. He, too, like the Vençois, is what history has made him, all the way back to the Cro-Magnon man and the dreamers of the New Stone Age. Unless he is an Oriental or an African or a red Indian, the American is the heir of all Europe's experience, the barbaric invasions, the plagues, the religious wars, the revolutions. They are in his blood, for if they did not happen to his forebears somewhere in southern France, then they stormed about his distant ancestry in some town of Holland, or Sweden, or Hungary, or England. You cannot get away from the accumulated suffering of mankind, or shake off the lesson that it should teach us.

And that lesson is that what goes on in my neighbor's house concerns me. If I let him go in need, I too may want. If he has an enemy, he will require me as a friend. If Nature is unkind to him, then I must be kinder. These are all simple things, known from time immemorial to any villager.

When the Germans deliberately destroyed the village of Lidice, an innocent community which had never even been at war with them, the indignation of the American people was swifter and deeper than when Warsaw or Rotterdam was destroyed. Perhaps that wasn't logical of us, but a village, like a family house, still has a sacred place in the heart. Upon the level of this unit of humanity, we are successful. And that a little town in Illinois should seize the name of fallen Lidice and take that for its own, so that the dead should live forever, is one of those strange, impractical, passionate small happenings that gleam like hope for the whole human race.

We need not wait for such a town as Vence to be razed, and its every inhabitant slaughtered, before we take it to our hearts as our own. The men of General Patch who took it, took it in the one right spirit—that it might be safe and free. You need not bleed in the streets of a foreign town to fight for it. You have but to rank it, neighborly, beside your own—your lilac-scented, gray-roofed New England village, your low, white-blazing desert hamlet of adobe, your plain, straight-streeted, honest town in the corn lands or the cotton lands. As the barons and the bishops and the quarreling kings fade out of my story of Vence, so are the dictators toppling, in the burning chapter of world history today. The people emerge triumphant, and the people—even in streets with an ocean running down the middle—must recognize one another as neighbors.

⟦ PRINTED
IN U·S·A ⟧

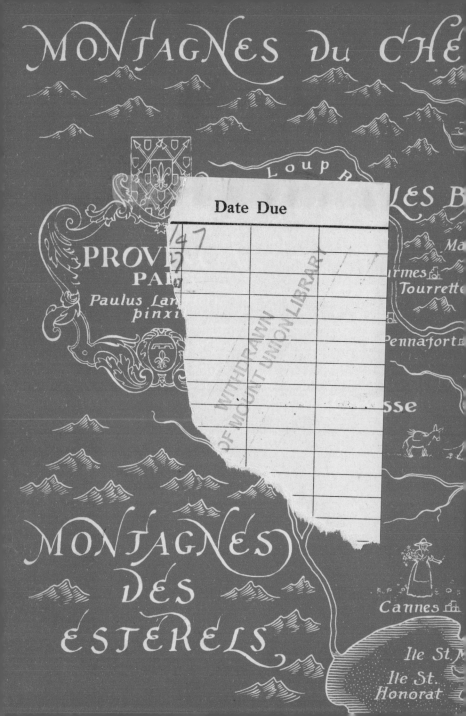

MONTAGNES DU CHE

Loup B

LES B

PROVE

PAR

Paulus Lar
pinxi

Ma

rmes

Tourrette

Pennafort

sse

MONTAGNES

DES

ESTERELS

Cannes

Ile St. M

Ile St.

Honorat